PRAISE FOR *VICTORY LA*

"This book truly resonated with me. I perso..... ...... 'Sudden
Retirement Syndrome' until I created my own Victory Lap. The
advice for achieving financial independence—Findependence—is
rock solid and essential to healthy, happy, later-life security. This is
a must-read for people of any age planning their life cycles."

—*Dr. Sherry Cooper, Chief Economist, Dominion Lending Centres;
Former Executive Vice-President and Chief Economist, BMO
Financial Group*

"You don't have to stop working in retirement. You can design an 'encore career' that keeps you from depleting your savings too soon and
provides an alternative to doing nothing. Boredom is the elephant in
the room, say Mike Drak and Jon Chevreau, who build on their own
experiences to help you embark on your own Victory Lap."

—*Ellen Roseman, personal finance journalist, author, continuing
education instructor, and Victory Lap enthusiast*

"I've long believed that the idea of retiring at sixty-five is as outdated as the horse and buggy. You could live another thirty years or
more. What are you going to do with that time? This book can help
you find the answers."

—*Gordon Pape, Bestselling Author and Publisher of* The Internet
Wealth Builder *and* The Income Investor

"Jon and Mike reframe the idea of retirement as a smart twist on an
age-old dilemma. The science of well-being later in life tells us we
need to have a purpose—why not make a few bucks while you're at
it? This book will open your mind to what your Victory Lap might
be if the thought of doing nothing at some point is foreign to you."

—*Larry Berman, Host of BNN's* Berman's Call, *and Chief
Investment Officer, ETF Capital Management*

"I've always believed once you have your financial house in order it
would free you up to do the things you love to do and would give
your life more meaning and balance. Imagine the luxury of working because you want to, not because you have to. No one wants life
to become a series of takeaways. Stay in the game. Enjoy and thrive
during your 'Victory Lap.'"

—*Patricia Lovett-Reid, Chief Financial Commentator, CTV News*

"A 'new age' approach to enjoying a more fulfilling and sustainable retirement lifestyle that you can embrace, customize and implement. Bravo!"
—*Daryl Diamond, Author of* Your Retirement Income Blueprint

"Too many of us treat financial independence as the end game but that's the wrong approach. Financial independence, or Findependence, should be seen as the start line of a new chapter of life. Rather than focusing on how to get to Findependence, *Victory Lap Retirement* focuses on life after Findependence and how to create and maintain a healthy, satisfying, and self-fulfilling lifestyle. Easy and informative to read, everyone working toward Findependence should read *Victory Lap Retirement.*"
—*Tawcan from* www.tawcan.com, *Early-Retirement Blogger*

"Chevreau and Drak have pulled off the informative and entertaining sequel to *Findependence Day—Victory Lap* is a fun book that everyone of all ages should read."
—*Diane Francis,* National Post *Editor-at-Large*

"Jon and I have had many stimulating discussions about our parallel 'working retirements.' I urge everyone to read *Victory Life Retirement* to discover how to achieve your own 'Findependence Day.' This will free you financially so you can embrace an encore career that will make you jump out of bed every morning with a smile on your face."
—*Sheryl Smolkin, Journalist, Pension Lawyer*

"Chevreau and Drak's primer on how to transition to retirement by outlining how to work while you play is full of helpful tips on how to align habits with long-term goals. You'll be richer for reading it."
—*Julie Cazzin, Senior Editor,* MoneySense

"Like pioneers documenting their personal journey into the new uncharted lands of redesigning retirement, Jonathan and Mike offer valuable insights and survival strategies to help properly prepare those who will follow in their quest to this new frontier."
—*Doug Dahmer, Founder, Emeritus Retirement Income Specialists*

VICTORY LAP RETIREMENT

Work While You Play, Play While You Work
The Joy of Financial Independence ... at Any Age

MIKE DRAK
JONATHAN CHEVREAU

MILNER &
ASSOCIATES INC
· EDITING · PUBLISHING · COMMUNICATIONS · CONSULTING

Library and Archives Canada Cataloguing in Publication Data

Drak, Mike, author
    Victory lap retirement : work while you play, play while you work—the joy of financial independence...at any age / Mike Drak and Jonathan Chevreau.

Issued in print and electronic formats.
ISBN 978-0-9939990-9-3 (paperback).—ISBN 978-1-988344-00-3 (html)

    1. Retirement—Planning.   2. Retirement income—Planning.
    3. Work-life balance.   4. Job satisfaction.
    I. Chevreau, Jonathan, author   II. Title.

HQ1062.D733 2016   646.7'9   C2016-902242-0
                                      C2016-902243-9

Production Credits
Editor and project manager: Karen Milner
Copy editor: Lindsay Humphreys
Technical editor: Chris Cottier
Interior design and typesetting: Adrian So, ADRIANSODESIGN.COM
Cover design: Adrian So, ADRIANSODESIGN.COM
Cartoons: Steve Nease
Printer: Friesens

Published by Milner & Associates Inc.
www.milnerassociates.ca

Printed in Canada
10 9 8 7 6 5 4 3 2 1

*To our fellow baby boomers. It's finally our turn again.
What are you waiting for?*

and

*To our kids, the millennials: use the lessons of Victory Lap
as a leg up and learn to play the long game on your terms.*

Contents

Foreword

by Ernie Zelinski

Having spent over half of my adult life in the business of personal development, mainly related to leisure and retirement, I have often been asked, "What is the secret to enjoying retirement to the fullest?" In other words, what can we do to make the years ahead of us satisfying and meaningful? To be sure, this is an important question. It is a particularly important question to ask ourselves as we approach the so-called retirement age. In fact, it's a worthwhile question to ask ourselves at any stage in life. Another key question is, "How can we transition from work to retirement in an easy and stress-free manner?" This is where *Victory Lap Retirement* valiantly enters the picture. It answers both questions by reawakening us to what truly matters in our lives and showing us the path toward creating a low stress, healthy, vibrant lifestyle.

Jonathan and Mike will help you rethink what retirement means to you, particularly if you tend to think of it in the traditional sense. After giving the subject of retirement some serious thought themselves, and also doing some intensive research on it, the two authors have come up with a new perspective on how to manifest your grandest desires, transitioning from your main career into a life of more leisure combined with satisfying pursuits.

An unknown wise person once proclaimed, "Retirement is wonderful if you have two essentials—much to live on and much to live for." The keys to attracting these two important elements of retirement are in the pages of this book. *Victory Lap Retirement* is not only for those considering their retirement but also for anyone interested in the pursuit of happiness, satisfaction, and self-actualization.

Many of the books and magazines that discuss retirement focus on building a nest egg, investing, and accumulating wealth. To be sure, this book offers helpful financial advice (in particular, I direct your attention to Jonathan's "seven eternal truths of financial independence" in chapter 4), but it comprises so much more than financial planning because the authors know that happiness during retirement is largely dependent upon other factors: having good health, good friends, and a variety of interests.

The traditional retirement-planning industry falls short on providing retirement-planning tools that help us realize what truly matters most about our lives and our retirement. The new retirement-planning model requires new styles of planning and preparedness, and that is what you'll find in *Victory Lap Retirement*. This masterpiece provides powerful tips, techniques, and secrets that can transform a boring, traditional retirement into an exciting one, including:

- How to put yourself firmly in command of your own financial destiny
- How to acquire wealth and how to manage it as it grows
- How to enjoy retirement regardless of your financial situation
- How to realize a deep new love for life
- How to free yourself from the burden of fearing traditional retirement
- The magic of the four-hour workday
- How to use your time wisely
- The importance of true freedom, which is not being imprisoned by money and material possessions
- What makes us happy, and focusing on that instead of on what wastes our time and energy
- How to give life to your dreams

If you have ever longed to have more, to experience more, to *be* more than you ever imagined being in your later years—possibly even more than you have ever been at any other time in your life—then *Victory Lap Retirement* is the book for you. The information and tools provided within its pages will vastly increase your chances of attaining the life you envision. The authors emphasize that retirement is not a time to rest. Retirement, instead, is a time to be active, to learn, and to explore; maybe even a time to start a new, fun career. Whether your finances allow you to travel or have a vacation home or require you to learn to live on less, you have many opportunities for living a decent and satisfying life.

In short, this book offers you a brilliant blueprint for enhancing your life financially, emotionally, intellectually, physically, and spiritually. It will inspire you still to be travelling, painting, taking photographs, and doing many other satisfying activities well into your seventies, eighties, and beyond, particularly if you still have good health. So allow Jonathan and Mike to lead you on a journey of self-discovery and renewal in the pages of this book, which will help make your life better than ever.

Ernie J. Zelinski
"Helping Adventurous Souls Live Prosperous and Free"
International best-selling author of *How to Retire Happy, Wild, and Free* (over 275,000 copies sold and published in nine languages) and *The Joy of Not Working* (over 285,000 copies sold and published in seventeen languages)

Preface

A Retirement Book about Not Retiring

by Mike Drak

I smile every time I think about the fact that Jonathan and I have written a retirement book about not retiring. I know it's weird, but weird seems to work in today's world.

It all started about five years ago: the day I woke up and realized I didn't want to do my corporate job anymore. Thinking like this was strange for me because I had always liked my job. I was good at it and it paid well, providing security and a good living for my family. But truth be told, over the last few years the job was starting to have a negative effect both on my health and on my personal well-being. The stress of performing at a high level year in and year out was getting to me. I was reminded of this every morning, when I took my blood pressure medication.

For a long time I hadn't been taking proper care of myself. I wasn't in a good spot mentally or physically and was out of balance. I had been so caught up in the competitions, titles, and salary increases along the way in my career that I had lost track of who I was in the process. I had bought into the idea that material success would eventually bring me happiness, but believe me on this, it doesn't! I really didn't know what would make me happy, I just knew that I didn't like how I felt anymore. I used to laugh a lot more and I didn't understand why that had stopped. I yearned to get rid of that nagging feeling and the sense that something needed to change. I had to slow down the pace of life and get out of the rat race.

But what was I going to do? Was retiring my only alternative? And if I did retire, to what would I be retiring? I had no idea, but I knew in my heart that a full-stop retirement just wasn't in the cards for me: I get bored easily and the thought of possibly spending more years in retirement, with nothing to do, than I had spent in my working life scared me a little—no, make that *a lot*. I didn't want my story to be, "He went to school, married, worked for a company for thirty-plus years while raising a family, then retired." I had worked and sacrificed too much over the years to have it all end abruptly like that. My corporate job had served its purpose, but I wasn't done yet and I knew my best days were still ahead. I wanted more—much more—out of life.

In my search for answers I visited the local library and read every retirement book I could get my hands on. Most of them were limited to the financial aspects of retirement. But then I was lucky to get my hands on a copy of Ernie Zelinski's book *How to Retire Happy, Wild, and Free: Retirement Wisdom that You Won't Get from Your Financial Advisor.* This is a must-read for anyone considering retirement. (Coincidentally, while I hadn't yet met Jonathan at the time, I recall seeing on the back cover of the book a blurb that he had contributed when he was a full-time columnist for the *Financial Post*.)

You won't find the usual focus on numbers in Zelinski's book because it deals with the emotional side of retirement, which was what I was really looking for. After finishing the book and following much reflection on my part, I knew that traditional retirement wasn't the answer for me. Instead I felt that it would be some combination of work and leisure that would make me happy and let me spend the rest of my life making good memories. Over time, this combination of work and leisure evolved into the concept of Victory Lap Retirement.

I got lucky again one day late in 2014. While surfing the Internet I came across Jonathan's work and the Financial Independence Hub, which everyone just calls the Hub. I realized that financial independence, or Findependence as Jonathan likes to call it, should be the cornerstone and prerequisite for Victory Lap Retirement. Once you have achieved some level of Findependence, you have the confidence to focus on creating a lifestyle that will work for you after leaving your primary career behind. First comes Findependence, then comes Victory Lap: so logical, so simple, so sweet! It made sense to approach Jonathan and ask him to join me in writing this book as, after all, he was the expert on Findependence. I was thrilled when he accepted my offer to work together.

With the steady increase in the average length of human life that is resulting from continuing advancements in science and medicine, we feel Victory Laps will become the new normal and replace that long-ago-created artificial retirement finish line. In Victory Lap there is no set finish line; you create your own race and enjoy every bit of it while it lasts.

• • •

The purpose of this book is to help people design a happy and fulfilling life for themselves; a lifestyle that reduces stress, reduces the demands attached to a full-time job and is based on a combination of work and play that can be carried on for as long as a person desires. Instead of running the rat race or being stuck on the treadmill of life, learn how you can break through the finish line of financial independence and plan your own Victory Lap.

When you finish this book, we encourage you to share it with someone you care about, perhaps your children or grandchildren so they can learn about the power of Findependence, or maybe another boomer who is still struggling with what to do with a life beyond employment. After all, we are all in this together!

We also welcome you to join our new Victory Lap community at www.victorylapretirement.ca, where there will be regular blogs on everything relating to creating and maintaining a successful Victory Lap. Hopefully you will consider joining in on the fun, as we can all learn more from each other. Please feel free to contact either of us and share your own stories:

michael.drak@yahoo.ca

or

jonathan@findependencehub.com

Introduction

Victory Lap Retirement and Findependence

Confession: we're on a bit of a crusade to change the way our society thinks about retirement. Jonathan has spent the better part of ten years trying to get the financial world to replace the word "retirement" with "Findependence" (short for financial independence). Then along came Mike Drak, with the complementary concept of the Victory Lap. Having spent most of his corporate career with two big banks, Mike now consults and speaks on life *in* retirement and is an evangelist for a new way of thinking about this phase of life, a time that can be more vibrant, liberating, and fulfilling than you ever imagined—a time we call Victory Lap Retirement.

A Victory Lap most commonly describes the slow, victorious circuit taken by an athlete of any track, playing field, or sheet of ice after winning a race or other sporting contest. It's that extra, happy time of continuing to run, bike, or skate, but it's done in a different way and at an entirely different pace. It's an opportunity to bask in the glory and enjoy the fruits of months or years of training, practice, and sacrifice.

A Victory Lap occurs after the main event, as it were. It's a continuation of a race or sporting event that's sort of the same as, but mostly different than, what came before. Similarly, our version of the concept, *Victory Lap Retirement*, refers to a new stage of life between the traditional salaried "primary" career and the end-game of "full-stop" retirement. You may continue to work after your full-time employment, but in a different way and at a different pace; and you'll be able to enjoy much more leisure time than at any time of your life before that.

When we first mention the Victory Lap concept, people often think of the Encore Act or Legacy Career promoted by organizations like Encore.org. While it's partly related to these ideas, Victory Lap Retirement encompasses much more. Whereas an encore career may consist solely of a new job in a new line of work, a Victory Lap is a complete, all-round lifestyle that each person designs intentionally for himself or herself. The idea is to create an ideal blend of work and play (hence this book's subtitle). You'll see from the table of contents that we also include chapters on health, time, and spiritual health, for example, in addition to chapters concerned with work and more strictly financial matters.

The benefits of the more holistic philosophy of Victory Lap Retirement are many. It can actually help to improve the overall quality of the rest of your life and, by extension, the lives of your loved ones. Who doesn't want to live a longer, healthier, and more productive life? Who doesn't want to manifest their innermost dreams and achieve goals long suppressed while spending decades raising a family and building wealth?

• • •

Older baby boomers may already be leaving corporate life in their late fifties or early sixties, but few are ready to hang up their skates and settle for a passive life of watching daytime television, playing golf, or—Jonathan's personal favourite—playing online bridge, for example.

The essence of Victory Lap Retirement is to leave corporate employment, which usually entails working for someone else, and enter a new and different phase of your life. This may mean working for yourself, but it could also simply mean continuing to keep the little grey cells active in some other way—hopefully in a way that supplements whatever pension and retirement income you've generated as a result of decades of "slaving and saving." In the end, it's about working because you *want* to, not because you *have* to (financially speaking).

No matter what kind of Victory Lap you envision for yourself, it should be built on a foundation of financial independence. We'd even go so far as to say Findependence is a prerequisite to pursuing a Victory Lap. Attaining financial independence by the time you're ready to leave the corporate world can free you to design a Victory Lap that's right for you.

At a minimum, being financially independent means being debt-free and having multiple streams of income—these may come from employer and/or government pensions, investments, part-time work, royalties or licenses, or perhaps business or Web income derived from entrepreneurial ventures on the Internet.

There's power in drawing a line in the sand and declaring that such-and-such is the exact day in the future you've picked to declare that your financial independence has arrived. That magical day is what Jonathan has coined Findependence Day. After that point, you may well continue to work just as you had before, but you would be working with the knowledge that you no longer *have* to, but *choose* to. You enjoy work for its own sake (what some call the "work optional" stage). It's a period in your life that should be fun, which is why Michael coined it Victory Lap.

• • •

The two ideas—Findependence and Victory Lap—complement each other; as you will see on page 40 in one of this book's illustrations by cartoonist Steve Nease, the Victory Lap begins just as you cross the Findependence Day finish line.

Make no mistake about it, establishing Findependence is a long-distance marathon that may take decades to achieve. It even took that long for Jonathan, who invented the concept and is a candidate for being the poster child for doing what you're supposed to in terms of maximizing savings and investments (see the seven eternal truths of financial independence in chapter 4).

Implicit in the world view of Victory Lap Retirement is the assumption of extended life expectancy. Thanks to continual advancements in medicine and the health sciences, it's more likely that we will live ten or twenty more years than we may have imagined when we first started our primary careers. Certainly the vibrant, healthy years of retirement could easily go into the nineties for many.

That's good news but all those extra years will cost a lot of money. The great thing about a post-corporate Victory Lap is you can pursue your passion or discover a new one, and get paid for it.

For younger people, the dream of a full-stop retirement is becoming less and less attainable. If the official "retirement" age keeps rising, young people being told to save for their old age will likely throw up their hands. They'll protest that it makes no sense to deny the younger versions of their selves so their older selves will have financial security half a century after their golden youth has passed.

We believe the concepts of Findependence and Victory Lap Retirement are much more alluring—and attainable—goals than the antiquated notion of full-stop retirement that the media and financial industry keep peddling. This book is aimed both at baby boomers and their "millennial" children, so they can design the life they want intentionally, no matter what stage they are at in the financial life cycle.

There are all kinds of Victory Lap Retirements. Some may pursue a traditional retirement but keep their hand in the workforce by working just a few days a week. Others may still choose to work for a salary but only on a part-time basis, strictly to generate what we call a "playcheque." That's a bit of extra fun money that can be spent guilt-free on little luxuries or experiences as opposed to accumulating more "stuff." For example, Jonathan's friend Meta is pushing 100 but still works two half days a week so she can take one-day excursions to attend plays or visit wineries. Others will make the leap from the corporate cubicle to self-employment.

However you choose to design your Victory Lap Retirement, it should provide a huge amount of flexibility compared to the nine-to-five corporate grind. You're now your own boss and can work as much or as little as you wish, as you craft a lifestyle that best combines the elements of work and play that appeal to your unique personality. Your days are now dictated by your personal passions and goals that you may have put off during your time in the cubicle. You may still be earning money, but what you're doing will be slightly or completely different than your old career. Odds are you will find this new phase of your life much more fulfilling.

• • •

But back to the illustration on page 40. At some point, you finally reach the finish line that brings an end to the long rat race of traditional employment. As you burst through the *Findependence Day* finish line, you've reached the end of the retirement-savings marathon. There's a smile on your face. Exhilaration. You still have some momentum, so you keep running past the tape, slowing down to a jog perhaps, taking time to savour the admiring crowd on either side of the track. They've been cheering you on and you bask in the glory, accepting a kiss here and a bottle of water there.

But you're so used to running all those years, it's hard to stop. So you don't. You adopt a slightly more comfortable pace and keep on jogging so more of your fans along the track can see you. You wave and smile, keep running and complete a Victory Lap. Or two or three.

That's what this book is about. You may have achieved financial independence or are close to it, but you need a better understanding of life *after* Findependence. For one, there are many technical issues, like decumulation (a.k.a. de-accumulation) or drawing down an income. And a key part of the planning process is goal-setting—envisioning the kind of Victory Lap that's right for you.

For findependent baby boomers, we believe the best is yet to come. In our own circles we can think of a financial adviser who has become an actor, a rock star who became an Anglican minister, and a pension expert who now runs a retirement website. Closer to home, at sixty, Jonathan's brother, Graham, put an ad on Kijiji to start his own rock band, Good Company. Oh, and most recently, a corporate banker turned author/blogger/platform speaker!

The boomers may be corporate refugees now, but few of us are ready to get off the track and plonk down in the easy chair for the rest of our lives. We may not be running flat out anymore or marching to the tune of some corporate boss half our age, but we're hardly done yet.

Welcome to Victory Lap Retirement!

1

Rethinking Retirement

It is not realistic to finance a 30-year retirement with 30 years of work.
You can't expect to put 10% of your income aside and then finance a
retirement that's just as long.
—John Shoven, Stanford University professor of economics

Today the word "retirement" is being widely misused and
fails to describe exactly what life looks like for people in
their fifties, sixties, seventies and beyond. To understand the
issue fully, it's helpful to look back on a brief history of retirement—how that system came to be, and what that way of life
typically has looked like.

Retirement as we know it today did not exist prior to the industrialization of various Western democracies. People lived on
farms just like on the television show *The Waltons*. Farmers didn't
retire, and the responsibility of older farmers was to pass on their
knowledge and skills to the next generation. In return, the sons
and daughters accepted the responsibility to provide care to the
elderly, which was payback for the parents raising them. Life was
a lot simpler back then.

Industrialization and the lure of a better life in cities resulted in people shifting from a life of self-sufficiency to a life of dependency on their employers. This shift came at a cost, as the new factory worker gave up a way of life that was in itself satisfying, trading a life where he was in control for a future where he would be a small cog in a large machine.

Along with industrialization came the eventual creation of Social Security in the United States. Launched in 1935, Social Security was designed to support the older worker who, on average, didn't have that many years left to live. The viability of Social Security counted on the assumption that the majority of retirees would die within a few years of starting retirement.

So everyone had the same goal: you worked hard for thirty-five years, and then, if you were one of the lucky ones to actually reach the finish line, you could finally stop working and enjoy a few years of passive leisure. We use the term "passive leisure" here, as most people back then were not in robust enough health to partake in active leisure. So it's easy to see why people would link "not working" to retirement, as it was the natural progression at the time: stop working = rocking chair. The literal definition of "retire" is to withdraw, to retreat, to shut oneself away. This definition was an appropriate fit for what was happening at that time.

Then a funny thing happened: people started to live longer. And they weren't just living longer, they were also healthier and more active in those later years. For evidence of this, visit any community recreation centre and you will be amazed at the number of baby boomers working out, taking aerobic or yoga classes, swimming, cycling, or lifting weights.

You hear of extreme examples all the time. In the March 16, 2015, edition of the *Toronto Star*, it was reported that Georgina Harwood celebrated her 100th birthday with a skydive. Let's just say that again—a *skydive*! After landing, she said she was going to follow it up with a shark-cage dive the week after. For Harwood, a great-grandmother, this was her third skydive. She executed her first when she was ninety-two years old in 2007.

Jaring Timmerman, a record-breaking swimmer from Winnipeg, Manitoba, died at the age of 105. Only a year earlier he had set Masters world records in both the 50-metre freestyle and 50-metre backstroke events.

PBS NewsHour economics correspondent, Paul Solman, told the story in 2013 of Vita Needle, an eighty-year-old company in Needham, Massachusetts. The average age of workers at the family-owned needle and tube manufacturer is seventy-four years. At the time of the PBS feature, the oldest employee was Rosa Finnegan, age 100, followed by Bill Ferson, age 94. Bob O'Mara, 78 years old, is a retired engineer who had worked at Vita Needle for eleven years.

This is just a tiny sample of what some "elderly" individuals are doing today. The question we need to ask ourselves is whether these people really retired, because it's pretty evident that they have not withdrawn or retreated. And if they are not retired, what are they?

Retirement is still a perfectly good word, but we need to rein in its usage now that its original meaning is no longer all that relevant because people are living longer, healthier, more active lives. So the challenge now is to find a word that is more befitting to that period of time between when people leave their primary career and when they land in the proverbial rocking chair during their latter years.

FROM RETIREMENT TO VICTORY LAP: A NEW STAGE OF LIVING

In his highly influential book first published in 1978, *The Three Boxes of Life: And How to Get Out of Them*, Richard N. Bolles described three life stages: education, work, and retirement. Each of the three boxes Bolles described was a different size, relative to how the typical North American's life was structured at the time the book was written. The biggest box was the work stage and the smallest was the third, based on the old definition of retirement, comprising people lucky enough to reach the artificial retirement finish line of 65. The reward for getting to the retirement box was being able to sit back and watch the world go by for a couple of years.

As stated earlier in the chapter, this framework for life worked fine until people started to live longer. Instead of a retirement stage lasting a few years, we are now looking at a stage that could last as long as, or longer than, a person's work stage. We think everyone would agree that's way too long to spend in a rocking chair! And some might also argue thirty or forty years is a long time to go without a paycheque.

To take into account the effect of increased longevity, it makes sense to insert a new box before the final one. We have chosen to call this new third stage "Victory Lap" in recognition of the increasingly common reality whereby people (often corporate or government employees) who eventually achieve financial independence (a.k.a. "Findependence") decide to pursue something more meaningful or, at least, choose to do the work they do differently.

People entering the Victory Lap stage are at a point when many of the primary responsibilities they once had have been eliminated or are down to greatly reduced and manageable levels. These responsibilities include helping the kids finance post-secondary education and leave home, eliminating all non–tax-deductible consumer debt (chiefly credit cards), and, ideally, paying off the mortgage or at least cutting it in half. Achieving financial independence gives people an opportunity to decide what to do with their newfound freedom. People now have options—options they haven't had for a very long time.

Believe us on this point: having options is a wonderful thing. Options make life interesting and allow you to be creative again, and following through on options makes you happy! That's why we like to call this very active stage of "retirement" your Victory Lap. You've crossed the finish line and left the world of working-to-make-a-living behind. You've conquered many of the financial hurdles of your younger years, and now you can leave the rat race and follow a path of your own choosing.

In your Victory Lap you can continue to work, but you have the luxury of choosing to do only work that gives you what you want. Money and security are no longer the main motivators, because financial independence has finally allowed you to make a change in your priorities. You can continue to work for money (if only part-time) or decide to volunteer more of your time to help the community at large. Or you may decide not to work at all and instead spend your time in active leisure, travelling and learning from new experiences and adventures. The key here is that in your Victory Lap you are still engaged: learning and growing, enjoying life to its fullest.

It's important for each of us to pause, reflect, and think about what it is we really want out of this stage of life. If we plan for it properly, this period of time could deliver more purpose and meaning than did our previous working life. If we choose to work during our Victory Lap, we are not working for the love or need of money, we are working for the love of work because it feels good. We are not just working but, rather, living again.

The goal in stage three, the Victory Lap, is to extend this period of freedom, living like a kid again for as long as possible and squeezing every ounce out of life. Instrumental to doing so are these factors: maintaining your physical and mental health, adopting a positive attitude, and ensuring that your financial plan is aligned with your life plan.

After all is said and done, there will come a time when we will finally "retire" to the fourth and final life stage. No longer capable of being independent, we will become dependent on others for care and support during our remaining years. Many of us are going through this stage with our parents right now and are learning first-hand the realities and challenges of eldercare. Let's agree to confine our talk of "retirement" to the final, less vibrant stage of life. Our focus is on helping you to plan for the time prior to that final stage; a Victory Lap that's fulfilling, flexible, energizing—exactly what we all dream about and work so hard to achieve.

THE FUTURE OF RETIREMENT

The world of retirement is changing rapidly, like never before. Because people are living longer, with hundred-year lifespans becoming commonplace, this will have a huge impact on how we view work, education, and retirement in the years ahead— especially as people are not just living longer, they are also more active and vibrant in their later years than used to be typical.

Recently we began a search for Victory Lap role models and bumped into the story of Professor Fred Kummerow, the driving force behind the fight to get trans fats out of our diets. After spending nearly sixty years writing about the link between trans fats and heart disease, and after starting a lawsuit against the U.S. Food and Drug Administration for failure to act upon his findings, Kummerow scored a major victory when the FDA made it a requirement for food companies to phase out the fats.

Professor Kummerow officially retired from the University of Illinois at age seventy-one but never quit working. He still maintains a lab at the university, and he was riding a bike to get there every day well into his eighties. He continues to be helped by two assistant professors who volunteer half their time, the balance being funded from Kummerow's own pocket and donations from charitable foundations. He is currently working on a project that will show the link between poor diets and Alzheimer's disease. To fund the new project, an application for a $1.8 million three-year grant has been made to the National Institute on Aging. Did we forget to mention that Professor Kummerow turned 101 when this book was published in 2016?

So living longer is a good thing, right? Maybe, but then again maybe not: it all depends on how you define living. In the greater scheme of things, the key is to understand that the trend of increased longevity is going to have a huge and profoundly disruptive impact on retirement, social, and workplace norms; we need to find ways to adapt successfully to this new environment.

Most of our current retirement thinking and assumptions are based on information we inherited from the twentieth century, and these old assumptions do not reflect the current reality. If you were twenty-two in 1973, you could expect to quite possibly be gone by age sixty-seven. But with life expectancy now up past eighty for Canadians, with Americans not far behind, the math doesn't work anymore. The old formula of working like a dog from age twenty to age sixty-five, then enjoying a few years of a happy retirement, no longer works. (Did it ever really work at all?) The fact is that many people will need to work longer.

But the arithmetic is not the only concern, as living longer isn't fun if most of those extra years are spent in poor health. We believe people need to adapt to the new reality if they wish to maximize the quality of life in their latter years. Work—the *right* work, for which you have a passion and that you love to do—can enhance your life and keep you active and engaged for a good chunk of those extra years. This book is intended to help you find that type of work, and as much or as little of it as is right for you, so that you can enjoy all the other good things in life.

The increase in longevity will also affect our kids, as what we refer to as their "workspans" (more on this in chapter 9) will need to increase at least as much as ours if not more. Therefore, this book is also intended to help them survive—and enjoy—a workspan that could last sixty years or more. This is a concern particularly for those who don't like their current jobs, deriving nothing from them but a paycheque (and one that's heavily taxed!). The next generation can use the Victory Lap philosophy to bypass entirely the corporate stage that most of us boomers endured during our formative years and instead create for themselves a long, sustainable workspan that's balanced by significant doses of fun and leisure. And so even the pre–Victory Lap workers of today can play while they work, and work while they play—and keep that model going many decades into the future.

Given that you and any kids you may have could have an extra thirty years of life, you can and should live your lives differently all the way through. The life stages leading up to Victory Lap could be lengthened: We could make young adulthood last longer. We could enter the workforce more gradually and exit more gradually. We could reach the peak of our careers in our sixties and seventies instead of in our forties and fifties. We could enjoy sabbaticals and mini-retirements during our working lives, in essence enjoying some of the freedom we traditionally defer to retirement long before we actually get there.

We are, in fact, talking about making that well-defined line between working and retirement a lot fuzzier—essentially mixing work and retirement for a long period of time. That is, in our working years we are enjoying some of what we would normally have put off for retirement; and when we normally would have retired, we are instead enjoying a Victory Lap—with a little bit (or as much as we want) of work and a lot of freedom to do and explore other things.

So as we say in our subtitle (*Work While you Play, Play While You Work*), in the Victory Lap the traditional distinction between work and leisure starts to fade. Increasingly, it becomes possible to structure our lives so that work often starts to resemble play and, as anyone who works at home well knows, play can often be interspersed with what we once would have considered "work."

WHY DO MEDIA SELL THE WRONG VERSION OF RETIREMENT?

Why does the advertising industry continue to sell us a version of retirement that doesn't reflect the current reality? For some strange reason, the financial media and financial services industries have not adjusted their traditional view of retirement to take into account the increased life expectancy and the changing demographics we've been describing. While this is puzzling, bankers are pretty smart, so surely they have a good reason for it. Or maybe their focus is on other things. Whatever the reason, they continue to sell the dream whereby, after working for several decades, one can finally enjoy a retirement that is filled with leisure and consumption.

You know the images, the ones that can be found in every second "retirement" advertisement: seemingly care-free, happy couples sitting on a beach in the Caribbean while sipping on a strawberry daiquiri, or perhaps they're sailing on a yacht, with the sun shining and the wind blowing through their hair as they embrace each other, smiling. Everything is perfect, perfect, perfect! And all of this could be yours if you only start saving a small amount of money each month. Or how about the other common image, in which a happy couple is playing golf on a picturesque course beside the ocean? You can almost hear the sound of the putt going into the hole for a birdie.

But when you stop to think about it, spending your next twenty years on a beach, a yacht, or a golf course is very expensive and probably out of reach for most people. That's especially so for those who have kids. According to *MoneySense* magazine, in Canada the average cost of raising a child to age eighteen is a whopping $243,660. That's $12,825 per child per year or $1,070 per month. And that's before you send them off to university! Taking this into account, it's simply unrealistic to expect that most of us will have millions of dollars on hand at age sixty-five.

Because the reality for most of us doesn't match what advertisers are telling us our "retirement" years should look like, it can cause us to feel anxiety and discouragement from knowing in our hearts that the vision is unobtainable. The financial services

"My Father told me that whoever dies with the most toys, wins."

industry doesn't help matters much either, as it creates the fear that we will not have enough in retirement to enjoy what they tell us we all deserve: the big house or vacation property, an expensive golf course membership, luxury cars, and exotic trips around the world. People who are trying to get us to buy their products or services have a tendency to make us feel we are not good enough unless we buy what the beautiful people are buying. They cast a spell, making us feel that something is always missing and that if we just had that one last thing everything would be okay.

That kind of thinking is just plain wrong. And wait, it gets worse, because even if you can afford the dream, odds are that, over time, you will become bored and disillusioned by it because it was never *your* dream—it was always *their* dream, planted in your mind! Truth be told, only a small portion of people identify with the idea of golfing or sailing in their later years, so the question should be, why do the retirement ads not reflect the current reality of retirement? The answer is simple: reality doesn't sell! Picture an ad depicting a grey-haired couple living in a small bungalow, each sitting in a different room. She's watching *The Price Is Right* and he's watching *Seinfeld* reruns on Netflix. The advertisement that shows them having dinner at Swiss Chalet or Denny's a couple of times a month just doesn't seem very glamorous, but it is the reality for many.

We believe that if you focus on designing the Victory Lap that's right for you, you can avoid falling prey to the advertisers' spell, thereby preventing yourself from feeling inadequate or frustrated if you can't attain what they think you should want and avoiding the life of penury and boredom to which many who lead a passive retirement are resigned. Somewhere between these two extremes you can plan and live the life beyond traditional work that *you* want.

MIKE ON BOREDOM

I remember when my family moved to a different part of the city when I was fifteen. There I was, at the beginning of summer, in a strange place with no friends and nothing to do, because I had missed the deadline for registration for baseball and other organized summer activities. So I spent the entire summer watching TV.

Eventually I became so in tune with the program schedules that I was able to tell the time of day or night by what show was on. Days drifted into weeks, weeks into months, and thankfully it was soon time to get back to school. How many kids do you know who are happy to go back to school? That's what boredom does to you!

It was a wasted summer, but it served me well because it provided a good taste of what real, sustained boredom is like.

> Boredom eats at your soul, and prolonged exposure to television actually has a numbing effect. After experiencing that, I made a promise to myself that I would never allow myself to go through another period like it again.

BOREDOM IN RETIREMENT: THE ELEPHANT IN THE ROOM

Unfortunately, for many people retirement is not much different from Mike's summer of endless TV watching, but for them the boredom lasts for years, not weeks and months, and it can literally be a killer. We all know by now the health benefits of an active lifestyle and, conversely, that a sedentary life increases health risks and takes years off your life—so yes, you really can die of boredom. When you think about the fact that many people spend some of what could be their best years watching TV because they can't afford to do something else or, worse, they can't think of anything else to do, it's hard not to get a little angry because we're doing this to ourselves; we are slowly dying inside if we choose a life of boredom.

There's no question that boredom isn't reserved only for people who can't afford to do other things. The reality is that any retirement based solely on one kind of activity—whether it be sitting on a beach somewhere drinking margaritas or golfing all day—usually ends in boredom. People need to be challenged constantly, and not just by who hits the longest drive. For this reason, boredom can be a living hell, no matter how much or how little that boring lifestyle costs.

Even in retirement you still need to get up each day, put clothes on, and find interesting, satisfying, and meaningful activities to fill the day. This period of your life could potentially last longer than the entire time you spent working, so you'd better think of some good ways to make your days challenging, stimulating, and rewarding. In chapter 5 we will help you find your *ikigai*, your reason to get out of bed in the morning.

A common misconception is that retirement is some Holy Grail whereby those who reach it become instantly happy and finally start enjoying life more. The truth is that if you weren't happy *before* retirement, the odds are that your life will not change much *in* retirement, and it could even turn out to be worse. The key for a happy retirement is to stay engaged, set challenging goals, and continue to take risks. For the co-authors of this book, continuing to work to some degree is important for our happiness. It keeps us busy and provides the fun money we need to finance the many adventures we've planned for our own Victory Laps.

WHY STOP WORKING? IT MIGHT KILL YOU!

Retirement kills more people than hard work ever did.

—*Malcolm Forbes*

Most people say when you get old you have to give things up, but I think we get old because we give things up.

—*Former U.S. Senator Theodore Green (who was ninety-eight when he retired in 1966!)*

Many people are starting to wake up and are realizing that the old version of retirement—saving for thirty years or more to fund a remaining period of leisure—just doesn't work for them. They are coming to understand that life was not meant to be a spectator sport and that watching TV for hours on end just won't cut it, especially as the average lifespan is increasing. People are concerned with how they are going to fill their days while they are still feeling healthy and active. How will they be able to afford such a long period of retirement? How can they maintain a satisfying and stress-free life? Folks are beginning to understand there is still so much more they can get out of life and that continuing to work in some capacity can play a big part in this.

While "retirees" may want to stay in the game workwise, they can now call the shots and do it on their own terms. They have finally reached a time when they are able to view work differently and they are no longer working solely because they need the money. This time around they are doing work for the sheer joy of it and because it gives them a reason to get out of bed with a smile each morning.

The thing is, once you have achieved financial independence, work *feels* different. You may have noticed that those who have achieved Findependence are the fun people to hang out with—they have a certain joie de vivre that can only come from working not because they *have* to but because they *want* to. They are doing things that may look like work to casual observers but to them really isn't. That's because the meaning of work is reversed for people who choose to remain active and engaged: they are accomplishing something that matters to them, and the financial reward is a happy by-product. Once you take the *need* for money out of the equation, work can be a wonderful source of happiness and freedom.

We believe that when people choose to delay retirement and instead continue to work in a job that they enjoy, on their own terms, they reap several benefits:

1. **Delaying retirement reduces financial anxiety.**
    The greatest fear many have is outliving their money. People are losing sleep over rising health-care costs and the erosive effects of inflation. Postponing full

retirement allows you to consider delaying when you
start to receive government benefits, which will pay off
greatly down the road. For example, in Canada if you
delayed taking CPP to age seventy you would receive 42
per cent more than if you had taken it at sixty-five, and
a similar dynamic is at work with Social Security in the
United States. Prolonging the amount of time you earn
an income will also allow you to continue to save for the
future and probably delay drawing from your retirement
savings, all while being better able to finance your
desired lifestyle in the meantime.

2. **Delaying retirement will help you live longer.**
    Numerous studies have shown that mortality rates
    improve with an older retirement age. A ninety-year
    study of 1,528 Americans called *The Longevity Project*
    showed that people who chose to delay retirement
    had much longer lives than their retired, golfing
    counterparts. The continually productive men and
    women lived significantly longer than their couch-
    sitting, TV-watching friends. "It wasn't the happiest
    or the most relaxed older participants who lived the
    longest," the authors wrote, "it was those who were
    most engaged in pursuing their goals." The evidence is
    clear: having a purpose, a reason for getting out of bed
    in the morning, knowing where you are going and being
    committed to, and focused on, getting there is going to
    make you live longer.

3. **Delaying retirement will keep you
    healthier for longer.**
    Staying in the work game keeps you vital, involved,
    and healthier because you have to use your mind and

body in order to work. Retiring early only increases the chances of entering a long period of intellectual atrophy and monotonous leisure.

4. **Delaying retirement will insulate you from boredom.**
   Boredom is dangerous, as it can lead to self-destructive behaviour that accelerates the aging process and increases the odds of a person having a short and unhappy retirement. Why spend all those years saving up for a long retirement, only to end up killing yourself through your behaviour? Don't settle for watching *Seinfeld* reruns all day when you are capable of so much more.

BEWARE OF SUDDEN RETIREMENT SYNDROME

As far as we know, sudden retirement syndrome is not a real medical condition, but it does describe the shock of withdrawal that can occur when a person suddenly ends their career. Sudden retirement syndrome can be brought on by downsizing, formal retirement, and other events; but no matter the cause, the shock of going unprepared from being engaged in a busy work life to doing absolutely nothing can be very stressful, fraught with risks, and in extreme cases can even result in premature death. We have all heard stories of people in retirement who lost their motivation to do much of anything, started drinking heavily, for example, and died soon after.

Deciding to retire (or experiencing having your company or manager make that decision for you) is one of the single biggest life changes a person can go through. When you think about it, it is a kind of loss. It could be a happy loss or a sad loss, but to be suddenly without something to which you de-voted so much of your life can result in a profound, personal inner loss. For some it will feel like a death of sorts: death of one's corporate identity.

Truth be told, retirement shock can be hell for many. You start to feel alone as the stress and anxiety builds; no one seems to understand what you are going through. Most of the people in your life can't help because they can't relate to you being unhappy that you don't have to go to work anymore. It just doesn't make sense to them.

Usually stress can be alleviated by removing external stressors, like a bad boss or excessive demands at work, but with sudden retirement syndrome there is no external stressor to remove, as the stress comes from within ourselves. And if we cannot find a way to manage this stress, depression will eventually set in, and depression is a very bad thing. It robs you of your energy, vitality, and self-esteem, and generally leads to poor health. With depression typically come an unrelenting sad mood, an absence of energy, problems of concentrating or remembering, a loss of interest in activities previously enjoyed, and difficulties with sleeping and eating.

Not everyone will experience sudden retirement syndrome, but for those who do it can be mitigated by a person's degree of preparedness. People need to be aware of the emotional challenges they are likely to face and prepare themselves, both financially and psychologically, for the unexpected. Essentially, what each person needs to do is create and maintain his or her own version of an escape pod in case of emergency—and this is where Victory Lap thinking comes in. There will always be some anxiety involved in leaving the Corp, but it will be much less stressful if you view leaving as an opportunity to be free again; to find purpose and rebuild yourself. If you are able to find something that can replace the loss, something that gets you excited, odds are you will find this period in your life to be one of the happiest.

WOULD WE BE SO OBSESSED WITH
RETIRING IF WE ENJOYED OUR JOBS?

We were surprised one day by the following headline: *Gallup Poll: 70% of Americans Hate Their Stupid Jobs.* The article described a Gallup 2013 State of the American Workplace study in which 70 per cent of those who participated described themselves as "disengaged" from their work. It's sad, isn't it, to think of so many people working in jobs they hate. No wonder the fantasy of complete retirement looks so appealing to so many. You can see why people convince themselves that the only answer is to grin and bear it until they have the opportunity to retire and leave that job they loathe once and for all.

So many of us, this book's co-authors included, bought into the idea that we need to sacrifice a good portion of our lives and chase after money so we can one day achieve security for the family. For the two of us, it went on for decades, in part a reflection of the good old Protestant work ethic, in part a concession to the practical responsibilities of being spouses and parents. But it's crazy to keep doing something you hate (or even merely dislike) just so you can eventually accumulate enough money to finally do what it is you really enjoy doing. The stress could end up killing you before you have a chance to enjoy the money for which you spent so many years working.

In 2014, findings were reported by Statistics Canada, which had followed a group of workers who were aged fifty to sixty-four when they left their jobs. Ten years later, most had gone back to work; just 32 per cent of the men and 36 per cent of the women had not. Among those who left their careers in their early sixties, the agency found that 47 per cent of the men and 41 per cent of the women were re-employed within the next ten years, and most had rejoined the workforce within a year or two.

Based on these findings, one might conclude that in all prob-
ability many of the workers had jumped into early retirement to
escape a job they disliked. However, once retired the participants
discovered that they needed more: not just more money, but also
the social interaction, structure, and feeling of accomplishment
and purpose that the workplace can provide.

The truth is, most of us would not be obsessed with retiring
if we had a job that we truly enjoyed and that we were doing for
the right reasons. We need to stop complaining about how unhappy we are and instead focus on how we can find something we
have always wanted to do, and do it on our own terms. How can
we invest our time, energy, and money to create the lifestyle that
we have always wanted? This is what each of us must determine
for ourselves.

•   •   •

It's clear that the traditional full-stop retirement model just
doesn't work anymore. While it's good news that we will be living
longer, this poses the challenge of figuring out how to make sure
that those additional years are well spent with minimal stress and
maximum satisfaction. Adopting a Victory Lap lifestyle will help
you to ensure that your later years are satisfying ones, because
in Victory Lap you are no longer defined by what you once did,
instead you become who you once were. It allows you to get back
that carefree feeling of your youth while at the same time benefit-
ting from the wisdom gained over a lifetime of experiences. This
book was written for the people who want more out of life, those
who want to spend the rest of their lives making great memories
while squeezing as much life as possible out of their remaining
years.

2

Welcome to the Corporate Jungle

Every morning in Africa, a gazelle wakes up. It knows that it must run faster than the fastest lion, or it will be killed. Every morning a lion wakes up. It knows that it must outrun the slowest gazelle, or it will starve to death. It doesn't matter whether you are a lion or a gazelle: when the sun comes up, you better be running.
— *African parable*

There is something very wrong with the work world today: it is far too common to find employees who are tired, overworked, stressed out, and living in fear of an uncertain future. As a result, people are eating too much, watching too much television, and complaining too much, often self-medicating with drugs and/or alcohol or taking prescription medication to cope with their distress. How can it be that in North America, one of the most prosperous societies in the world, people are taking more medications for anxiety, depression, and sleep disorders than ever before?

As a population we are out of balance; our quality of life is being adversely affected and work is playing a significant role in what is happening. The societal norm is to focus on developing a career and becoming prosperous at the expense of everything else, even our families and our health. We have become consumed by work, and this is not a good thing.

STARTING ON THE WRONG FOOT

Throughout most of our lives we are told what to do, and therein lies the problem. It begins with the direction given to us by the education system and our parents. We are taught from an early age that the purpose of working hard and getting good grades is so that we will be able to get a good job that pays lots of money. With few exceptions, everything we were told was linked to the future and the goal of making more money. This is dangerous thinking, as you end up always trying to get somewhere other than where you are, forever chasing more money. You are never truly satisfied, as you are always focused on becoming, achieving, and attaining. This way of thinking creates stress, and stress over a prolonged period is harmful to our minds and bodies.

When a person starts a corporate career, he or she makes a deal with the Corp, trading personal freedom and dreams for money and the promise of security. The Corp says, "Do what you are told and work hard, and we will provide you and your family with a good living. If you continue to play ball and be a good soldier, in forty years you will retire with an excellent pension and a beautiful home fully paid for."

The corporate world's definition of success is programmed into our heads from day one, and it's fueled by the continual enticement of wealth, status, and the accumulation of material goods. We were taught the importance of following our bosses' orders; if we conformed and became a productive part of the organization, we were rewarded with prizes and shiny trinkets (which, in Mike's case, now fill up a significant part of his garage). The lure of these trinkets and prizes causes us to forget that true happiness is derived from achieving our dreams, attaining our personal goals, and having a loving family.

For those of us who accepted the corporate agreement, for a period of time everything worked out the way it was supposed to. But the Corp demanded a high price for its promises of safety and wealth. It demanded that we give up who we were, become compliant and obedient, and accept its version of the dream. We kept our part of the bargain for as long as we could, but eventually people's needs change and some of us can't keep the bargain any more. Blame it on Maslow.

MASLOW AND THE CORPORATE WORLD

If you plan on being anything less than you are capable of being, you will probably be unhappy all the days of your life.
—*Abraham Maslow*

Abraham Maslow was a psychologist who published a seminal paper in 1943 called "A Theory of Human Motivation." Maslow believed people are motivated to take care of certain needs and that when one need is fulfilled a person seeks to fulfill the next one, and so on. His famous "hierarchy of needs" theory consists of the following five levels:

1. Physiological needs: food, water, shelter, sleep
2. Safety needs: protection from the elements security, stability, protection
3. Love and belongingness needs: friendship, camaraderie, love, affection
4. Esteem needs: achievement, mastery, status, dominance, prestige, self-respect, respect from others
5. Self-actualization needs: realizing personal potential, self-fulfillment, seeking personal growth and peak experiences, helping others, sensing that you are doing what you are most fitted for

Once the first four levels are satisfied, Maslow theorized, those needs would no longer have the power to motivate us and people would feel discontented unless they experienced self-actualization or, as we like to call it, self-intentionalization.

Throughout our university years, we tend to rank high on the Maslow scale. Our physiological needs are being met: we have food and shelter, whether we are living in residence or are still in the family home. Our self-esteem needs are being met, as at this point in our lives the world is full of possibilities and we feel good about ourselves and our future.

During those early years, according to Maslow, we would rank just below the self-actualization level. But things change after you move out of the house, land a corporate job, and start your own family. Suddenly you find yourself near the bottom of the Maslow scale: most of your attention becomes focused on protecting your family, paying off the mortgage, and saving for eventual retirement.

When you join a corporation you are, in effect, making an informal agreement that you are willing to give over your life to the Corp in exchange for security for your family. It sounds harsh, but that's the reality for most of us. Many of us are wired to succeed, win awards, and earn promotions. The pressure to produce outstanding individual performance in a competitive environment leads to long hours and hard work. As a result, we end up spending most of our time at work or thinking about work. In doing so, we sacrifice our personal freedom to be who we really are. Indeed, some people so strongly identify with the Corp that the corporate roles they play can take over and essentially become who they are, and not being true to your own nature is not healthy in the long run.

THE TRAP

While it's possible for people at all levels within the Corp to feel a significant measure of mastery, fulfillment, personal growth, and self-fulfillment—those higher-level needs that Maslow talked about—the trade-off is that we often have a financial dependency on the Corp. This dependency is exacerbated by the rising costs of family life in the form of mortgages, cars, clothes, and kids. At a certain point we are driven into complete economic dependency through debt, new family needs, and consumerism.

This is when the fear starts to creep in. Salaries and bonuses may keep rising, but lifestyle inflation outpaces them, resulting in more consumption and more debt. That deepens the dependency, which then deepens the fear of job loss. It's a vicious circle, and before you know it you're trapped. You essentially give up your personal freedom in exchange for economic security, which is not even guaranteed. One day you realize the rules have changed and that working for the Corp is no longer a safe bet: people are in full-blown survivor mode trying to navigate the now-commonplace restructurings, downsizing, and mergers. Even long-term boomer employees and those with outstanding track records can end up on the chopping block. "That's business," as corporate bosses are fond of saying.

Even if you do reach a point when you start to feel financially secure, at the same time you might realize that your career no longer delivers the meaning you thought it would. Yet you spend your precious time working at a job that no longer excites you, with people you don't care much about, all for the sake of a little more money, and it causes you to die a little bit each day. You find yourself sitting at work, glancing now and then at your pension statement, trying to hang on so that you can maximize your payout and then finally begin enjoying life.

Perhaps you allowed yourself to be seduced and sucked into someone else's definition of success, until the day you wake up and think to yourself, "Hey, what happened to my life? It wasn't supposed to be this way!" While your material standard of living may be at an all-time high, your quality of life may be at an all-time low.

Why do so many of us decide to stay with the Corp, remain unhappy, and go on suffering? Well, by this point in our lives we have invested so much time and energy chasing financial security that it's hard to take a different tack and try something else. Learning to do something new later in life is just too scary for a lot of people: we often lack the confidence in ourselves to succeed; the perceived risk is just too great. People reason to themselves, why walk away from the twenty years that were invested in the Corp? But we think the real question should be, why waste the *next* twenty years doing something you dislike?

Job intensity has ramped up over the years, and today it seems like most people are just trying to find ways to keep up the pace. Years ago, jobs in most corporations had built-in seasonality; there was some downtime at some point. Today, however, it's pedal to the metal and business lulls are a thing of the past; managers track your sales results hourly, and every day is a

Ted was always afraid that one day the work zombies would finally get him.

competition with your co-workers. It reminds us of the oft-cited imagery of frogs in a pot of water on a stove, and in this case it is management that's turning up the temperature slowly so that nobody notices how hot it is until it's too late.

We end up going home at the end of the workday physically and mentally drained, with nothing left to give to our families. The best part of our day often consists of sitting down in front of the TV, rewarding ourselves with snacks and a drink (or three) for having survived another day. No matter how much money we make, status we have earned, or power we hold, we have allowed ourselves to become prisoners of the corporate institution.

The concept of institutionalism is well-defined in the movie *The Shawshank Redemption* (adapted from the novella written by Stephen King), which depicts life in a federal prison in the 1940s and 50s. As it's portrayed, the system was designed to stamp out any hope of freedom for its prisoners. The character Red, who's played by Morgan Freeman, has some particularly insightful lines about what it means to be institutionalized:

> *These walls are funny. First you hate 'em, then you get used to 'em. Enough time passes, you get so you depend on them. That's institutionalized. They send you here for life, that's exactly what they take. The part that counts anyway.*

The effects of incarceration on Shawshank Prison's long-term inmates are not unlike the effects of working in the corporate world, which is an institution in itself. Early in the movie, Brooks, who was a prisoner for over fifty years, discovers he will soon be set free; however, because he is so accustomed to the routines that have been long established for him, rather than be thrilled by this news, he's haunted by the realization that he will be unable to function in the real world and survive. As Red put it, "In here he's somebody, out there he's nobody." Soon after being released, Brooks commits suicide because he is unable to cope with change and life outside the prison institution.

Another prisoner, Andy, recognizes early on the importance of remaining tied to his life outside the walls, to have hope and to live for something, or else life isn't worth living. Andy refuses to sit in his cell for eighty years and wait to die. The hope of one day returning to the outside world is what motivates him to spend twenty years digging a tunnel to escape by crawling through a septic pipe.

START DIGGING YOUR ESCAPE TUNNEL

When you think about it in broader terms, you can see how the Corp can institutionalize you just as surely as Shawshank Prison did its inmates—but only if you allow it to. The smart ones among us do as Andy does and start digging their escape tunnel toward freedom (Findependence) the minute they join the Corp. They view the time they spend in the Corp as part of a bigger plan, adopting the institution purposefully and using the benefits it provides to help them reach their long-term goals.

Working toward financial independence and an eventual Victory Lap will give you hope and comfort, secure in the knowledge that you will one day get back control over your life, your future, and your time. Instead of focusing on how the Corp uses you, look at it in a different fashion: How are you using the Corp to meet your goal of Findependence?

If you haven't already started, you need to begin planning today for your "jailbreak" by creating your own destiny and charting your eventual Victory Lap. You really don't have another choice if you want to stay sane. It's crazy to stay in a job that no longer satisfies you, forever living with the fear of one day being forced out and being replaced by a younger, cheaper model.

HAVE YOU SERVED YOUR TIME?

It just doesn't stand to reason: why would you do stuff you don't like for more than thirty years, just so you can cash in on a pension or your retirement savings at the end? (And that's assuming you even make it to the end.) After a certain point, you must decide whether to keep your head down for a few more years in a job you hate or that's killing you with stress, or take a pay cut to work at something you could love doing for the rest of your days. Staying with the Corp and continuing to save for a supposedly successful retirement primarily for the sake of buying more things doesn't make sense if the prolonged stress of your job could cut your retirement life in half.

It's hard to understand why people feel they need to remain in prison even though the door is unlocked. Brooks had no choice, but we do, so why do so many of us choose to be imprisoned by our work? Problems arise when we stop putting our whole heart into life. The moment boredom rules our life, something dies within us. But despite unhappy circumstances, people rarely take the initiative to change their situation. Over the years they become conditioned to a life of security and conformity. This may appear to provide peace of mind, but in reality nothing is more damaging to a person's present quality of life than a secure future. The core of a person's spirit is passion for adventure. The joy of life comes from our encounters with new experiences, so it's important to accept change as a key part of our lives. Don't let your life spark be extinguished. Disengaged employees who waste their lives in unenjoyable dead-end jobs aren't making a living, they're making a dying!

Understand at the outset that the role of the Corp is to serve as a stepping stone to achieving the goal of financial freedom, and once you reach that goal your shackles will no longer exist. You will be free to decide whether to stay with the Corp or leave and create a Victory Lap lifestyle that is more meaningful and that will deliver on all your higher-level needs. It is a decision that can be in your control and on your terms if you have attained Findependence.

Leaving a high-paying job late in life is a risk, no question; but staying in a job you detest and hanging on to the end is a far bigger risk. We can't guarantee that opting to do a Victory Lap will be painless, but we *can* guarantee that it'll be less painful than regretting what might have happened if you had only taken the chance to make a change when the opportunity was there.

It's always easy to find a reason to stay put, do nothing, and not take a risk. So decide in advance, right now, to quit your present job someday. Create your exit plan for the day you will stop working for someone else and begin working for yourself. Make a list of what you'll need to do in order to make it happen—to break out of the Corp and start your own version of a Victory Lap, which will allow you to find happiness, fulfillment, and security on your own terms. Believe in yourself and know that you are smart enough, talented enough, and motivated enough to succeed in this crucial new stage of your life. Reduce your material needs and adopt a more frugal lifestyle. Get healthy. Start now!

• • •

For the record, we do not want to appear overly negative about working in the corporate world. When we set out to write this chapter, we were so focused on warning people about the dangers of working in the corporate jungle that we initially ignored many of the positive benefits that Corps can provide.

Looking back at our own multi-decade corporate careers, we both agree work was fun for a while and we were both good at it. We earned good money and it helped us achieve many of our goals. We were able to pay off our mortgages, raise the kids, help pay for their education, and achieve financial independence. Mike even had the added fortune of meeting his wife (whom he affectionately calls "the Contessa") at work, so you could say working at a Corp paid off in more ways than one. But like everything in life, the benefits of working in an organization come at a cost. It's this cost that we feel most people are not truly aware of, and that's why we felt we needed to point it out.

So let's say it again: it's crazy to work in a job you no longer enjoy just so you can save more money for a retirement about which you have no idea. You need to create a long-term plan and design a Victory Lap that will deliver to you the lifestyle that you always dreamed about. The rest of the book is designed to help you do exactly that.

Findependence

The Cornerstone of Victory Lap Retirement

To allow me to do what I want to do every day.
—Warren Buffett on what money means to him

We can't emphasize enough the importance of recognizing the power of financial independence and the instrumental part it can play in your life once it is achieved. Findependence is critical to creating the kind of Victory Lap that you want for yourself. Having complete financial freedom is what allows you to work and live on your own terms, doing what you want to do with your time and energy, not what someone else on whom you are financially dependent says you *have* to do in order to fulfill your financial obligations. So if Findependence is the key to a victorious (if you will) Victory Lap, how exactly do you work toward crossing the finish line of financial freedom?

First you must dismiss the outdated way of thinking pushed by the financial services industry, which continues to focus on the traditional "full-stop" retirement. This typically features "slaving and saving" in full-time salaried employment from age twenty to sixty-five, followed abruptly by a decade or two of what amounts to a permanent vacation.

Compounding the problem is the lack of financial education our children receive in school. So most people just default to saving more (or trying to save more, or being stressed that they can't save more no matter how hard they try), assuming the more money they save the better off their retirement will be; this may seem reasonable, but it's not always true. Instead of just blindly saving as much as you possibly can during your working years, assuming that the more you have the better off you'll be, what you must understand is that financial planning fails without *life* planning. The fact is, most people don't understand what they are actually saving *for*. We will get into the details of effective life planning later in the book; for now, it's something to keep in mind as we look at exactly what Findependence means and how you can plan to achieve it.

HOW DO I KNOW WHEN I'M FINDEPENDENT?

Findependence is best described on a cash-flow basis. It's the point where your basic (non-discretionary) living expenses are covered by your passive (non-work) income. This is the amount of annual cash flow you require to keep a roof over your head, put food on the table, and pay for the basic necessities (heating, electricity, property taxes, etc.).

The day you achieve Findependence is the day you no longer need to work in order to survive. That day (a.k.a. *Findependence Day*) is best described by the following formula:

PASSIVE INCOME > NON-DISCRETIONARY EXPENSES = FREEDOM

Let's take a simple example. Say your annual non-discretionary living expenses are $30,000. That means you would need to generate $30,000 in annual after-tax passive (non-work) income in order to be findependent.

Examples of passive (non-work) income sources include:
- Dividend and interest income from your investments
- Company pensions and government pensions
- Rental income from real estate investments
- Royalties from intellectual properties, books, music, apps

Defining Findependence this way means you won't require the millions of dollars in capital that some financial gurus insist you will need in order to create a happy "retirement." This is because you are now concerned only with covering your basic survival costs. Your discretionary costs that allow you to live a lifestyle beyond a survival lifestyle—money spent on entertainment, vacations and travel, eating out, club memberships, booze, and other luxuries—will be covered from the extra money you earn during your Victory Lap (part-time work, business income, etc.). If you're lucky enough or have worked and saved hard enough in your career, your passive income may even cover some or all of your discretionary expenses as well, giving you even more freedom and security in your Victory Lap years. But isn't it good to know that even if this isn't the case for you, at least Findependence will mean that you can work on your own terms, if you choose to work at all?

One way to track your progress toward Findependence is by calculating your Freedom Ratio, often described on the Retireby40.org website as follows:

FREEDOM RATIO (FR) =
AFTER-TAX PASSIVE INCOME/NON-DISCRETIONARY LIVING EXPENSES

For example, say your after-tax passive income is $20,000 and your non-discretionary living expenses total $40,000. In this case, your Freedom Ratio suggests you are halfway to your Findependence Day, which we would define as being a Freedom Ratio of 100 per cent. It follows that your goal would be to get the ratio up to 100 per cent as soon as possible, which would be achieved by doubling your passive income to $40,000. The alternative route would be extreme or "guerrilla" frugality, cutting your living expenses in half to achieve complete Findependence. Either method would yield a ratio of 100 per cent, although most North Americans would probably choose to boost their passive income rather than cut their cost of living.

In *The Intelligent Investor: The Definitive Book on Value Investing*, author Benjamin Graham discusses the concept of a "margin of safety," the difference between the price of a stock and its intrinsic value. The idea is that if a stock is priced lower than it is valued, owning that stock will give investors protection from volatility and market downturns. We believe it is prudent to maintain a margin of safety while in Victory Lap as well, maintaining a Freedom Ratio in excess of 100 per cent. This margin of safety would provide protection against future risks, such as the risk of inflation (real and lifestyle) and a possible drop in passive income levels due, for example, to a cut in a company's stock dividend.

If you can maintain this margin of safety for yourself, by keeping your passive income above your non-discretionary living expenses, the added benefit will be that you will have to rely less on other sources of income while you are enjoying your Victory Lap. If your discretionary spending (or at least some of it) is covered by your passive income, then you can truly work for the love of it rather than because you need the money. Or, under these happy circumstances, you may choose not to work for money at all.

While working toward Findependence, you really have only two variables to play with: active (work) income and living expenses. If your goal is to accelerate the arrival of your Findependence Day, it's important to adopt a frugal lifestyle and focus on increasing active income as much as possible via raises or promotions or perhaps by taking a second job.

It's important to review the numbers annually and make adjustments as you go along. You need to remain vigilant about the effects of inflation: Findependence could slip away over time, becoming an elusive goal if the costs of living rise faster than the passive income derived from your investments. Given the rampant printing of money by the world's central banks, inflation is not something you can easily dismiss.

At some point in their sixties, most Americans will start collecting Social Security, while Canadians will start receiving payments through the Canada Pension Plan (CPP), Old Age Security (OAS), and (for those with no other income sources) the Guaranteed Income Supplement (GIS). Some authors, such as Frederick Vettese in *The Essential Retirement Guide: A Contrarian's Perspective*, have taken to using the term Social Security even for the Canadian equivalent (CPP/OAS/GIS).

Whatever terms you use for the government benefits, these income sources will increase the amount of passive income you receive and, in turn, help you to maintain your Findependence. Also, you may decide at some point to draw down some of your investment capital to boost your income after you have left full-time employment behind (in which case, sorry, kids!).

Financial freedom is incredibly liberating, opening up a world of possibilities to you for how you want to live during your Victory Lap. Plan well in advance for your financial independence, declare your own Findependence Day, and start designing the kind of Victory Lap you want to run after you burst through that finish line. It's all under your control.

BENEFITS OF FINDEPENDENCE

There are many benefits of achieving Findependence. Here are three of the top ones:

1. You have earned the freedom to leave the protection of the corporate world and seek out work that's less stressful, more flexible, and more meaningful. Findependence gives you freedom of choice. You're no longer focused solely on making more money; instead, you're more focused on doing things that interest and matter to you.

2. Findependence is the ultimate safety net and gives you
    financial peace of mind. If you were to lose your job
    tomorrow you would be able to sleep at night, knowing
    your family will survive. You no longer have to worry
    about being able to pay your bills.

3. Achieving Findependence is a great booster of self-
    esteem. In the workplace you can usually spot the
    workers who have already achieved Findependence.
    They're the ones who speak up and say what they
    think without fear of getting fired. They know they
    are financially independent and that they will survive
    regardless of the fallout.

THE SIX STAGES OF THE FINANCIAL LIFE CYCLE

If you are going to plan to be findependent (and obviously we
strongly endorse this as a worthy goal), then you need to start
early in life, particularly if you want your Findependence Day
to come sooner rather than later. To this end, it's useful to take
a step back and look at the bigger picture of your financial life
cycle, to see where and how planning for financial freedom fits in.

As human beings we all go through predictable life stages:
we start off as infants, grow up, plateau for a time in adulthood,
become grey and feeble, and eventually shuffle off this mortal
coil. In similar fashion, and proceeding largely in parallel to the
physical development of human beings, there is a financial life
cycle. The Financial Independence Hub organizes its blogs into
six stages it has identified as comprising the human financial life
cycle, which we will outline for you here.

Rather than starting at infancy, however, we start the financial life cycle around age eighteen. At that point, we are in effect

"financial babies," with plenty of human capital (potential for future earnings) but very little financial capital. As we proceed through life's inevitable stages, we attempt to exchange our human capital for financial capital. That's because one day we won't be able to work for money, which is why everyone is nagging you about saving for retirement. Of course, in this book we won't nag you to save for retirement; instead we make the case for saving for financial independence. By now, you know the difference, right?

If you're a North American baby boomer approaching or considering embarking on traditional retirement, we'll assume you've already experienced the first three stages of the financial life cycle, so you can skip to stage four below. But we've included the whole cycle, since many boomer parents may want to pass this book on to their millennial or Generation X offspring.

Stage 1: Debt and Frugality

We envisage the human financial life cycle as beginning upon graduation from college, university, or technical training. Most likely, recent graduates entering the workforce for the first time will be in debt mode, emerging with a degree of some sort and student loans to pay off, and/or significant credit-card debt.

Job one is to dig yourself out of debt. By definition, you're nowhere near Findependence when you graduate from college or other educational institutions, since you likely have a negative net worth. Not only are you not ready to cross the Findependence finish line, you're really not even on the racetrack yet!

To pay down that debt, you'll have to practice what we call "guerrilla frugality" (more on this below). Also refer to the seven eternal truths of financial independence in the following chapter and you'll see that the first and most important truth is to live within your means. This means consistently spending less than you earn, year in and year out.

Ideally, at this stage we suggest aiming to save between 10 and 20 per cent of your after-tax income and investing it wisely, but that's not always possible, depending on your circumstances. Clearly, if you spend 100 per cent of what you earn, you're merely treading water and if you're in debt, you're sinking. As Didi, the fictional financial reality TV host in Jonathan's novel *Findependence Day*, puts it, "You can't climb the tower of wealth while mired in the basement of debt."

The only way to fight back is with guerrilla frugality. Why the term *guerrilla*? Because it's a jungle out there and the marketers and advertisers can be likened to practicing guerrilla marketing (or guerrilla warfare) on consumers. You'll have to fight back against the temptations they are constantly throwing in your way if you're to have any hope of eliminating your debt and starting to save toward your Findependence. Be frugal till it hurts; resist the blandishments of the TV and Web advertisements; ask yourself the question, "Do I really need this?" and keep answering, "No!" When you find yourself weakening, try the slogan that Didi suggests should be emblazoned on debtors' foreheads: "Freedom, not stuff!"

Remember, "stuff" ends up owning you, not the other way around. Keep the end goal in mind, which is financial freedom.

Stage 2: Family Formation and Housing

On to the second stage, which also requires continued attention to frugality. Sooner or later the big life event happens, whether in college or early in your work life: you meet that special someone and the next thing you know you're moving in together or exchanging "I do's" at a church or civil ceremony. With marriage typically comes (sooner or later) children and a home mortgage. We would argue "marriage, mortgage, and kids" are a holy triumvirate and that this is a key stage in the financial life cycle.

It's going to be a challenge now, especially if one spouse stops working to stay at home to raise the kids, but guerrilla frugality must continue in this stage. Hopefully you've eliminated your student loans and your high-interest credit-card debt, but if you have a large home mortgage, you may still have a negative net worth. Keep being frugal, keep living within your means, and pay down that mortgage. Ideally, you bought a sensible starter home in a reasonable area and the carrying costs aren't onerous. And you made as large a down payment as you could come up with, even if you had to tap the parents to do so.

Really, the Findependence game only begins when you've paid off the mortgage. Once you own your home free and clear, you will experience the exhilaration of knowing you have now laid the foundation of your future financial independence: a home that's fully paid for. No more worrying about making next month's payment!

Stage 3: Wealth Accumulation

By this stage, you may have dug yourself out of the basement of debt but most likely still have zero net worth. While you may no longer be in the red, there's still a long way to go before you're even close to being financially independent. Welcome to the long, long stage of building wealth in earnest.

Ideally, this stage will begin with your first job and pre-authorized automatic savings, although that isn't always possible. Down the road, once the mortgage is paid off, you can double down on saving for your Findependence: just divert the amount that had been going toward the mortgage to your retirement kitty! And notice that frugality is key to all these early stages: you need to be frugal to pay off debt, whether it be credit cards or a mortgage, and that habit of frugality is the same one required to build wealth. (See the next chapter for the seven eternal truths of financial independence, one of which is living within your means.)

For many modern couples, the building-wealth stage could easily last thirty or more years. This is the sweet spot for the financial services industry, which will be urging you to save and save some more, investing wisely in a variety of tax-sheltered plans and taxable investments. If you're employed and have a pension, this stage may occur almost automatically and perhaps painlessly, provided that you hang in for a decade or three. Note, too, that wealth accumulation is the flipside of decumulation and downsizing, which we will describe a little farther on.

Stage 4: Encore Acts (Victory Lap)

With the Victory Lap paradigm, there comes a time when one decides to leave corporate life. This may happen in one's fifties or early sixties. It may be voluntary or it may be at the instigation of your employer, who may decide you're getting too old and too expensive for their bottom line and that you should be replaced with a younger, cheaper model. Either way, by now you should have established at least a baseline of financial independence; maybe not enough for a 365-day-a-year permanent vacation, but by now you should have a certain amount of financial flexibility.

You have now reached the stage of the encore career or encore act. For some, this is a stage of the Victory Lap where you give back through volunteering and philanthropy, but it can also mean embarking on a brand new career path. It's time to put into motion your innermost dreams and long-suppressed life goals. No longer do you wish to be a salaried implementer of someone else's grand vision; now you want to be the star of your own show.

If you're building a business, ultimately it might be sold, in which case you are continuing to accumulate wealth (although it may not appear that way because any possible exit event may still be years or decades away). And if you are simply doing part-time or contract work, then you are supplementing your passive sources of income (such as pensions and income from investments). In either case, your encore act can boost your financial flexibility and, if you haven't already reached it, help you to reach your Findependence Day.

Stage 5: Decumulation and Downsizing

Closely tied to the encore stage, and sometimes coinciding with it in parallel, is the stage we call decumulation and downsizing. Even if your encore career is bringing in revenue, or has the potential to do so, in this stage you will be focused less on accumulating even more wealth and instead you will start planning for how to draw down some of the wealth you've so prudently accumulated over the prior decades.

The skillset for decumulation is quite different than wealth accumulation. You may find that the financial adviser who helped get you to Findependence may not be as well equipped for the decumulation phase. At this point in your life, it's not just about investing in things like stocks, bonds, investment funds, real estate investment trusts (REITs), or income trusts and holding for the long run. You now have to worry about drawing income in a tax-efficient manner and from a variety of income sources. Remember, the single biggest expense in retirement is likely to be taxes!

Notice, too, that just as the mirror image of wealth accumulation is decumulation, the mirror image of home ownership is downsizing. Back in Stage 2: Family Formation and Housing, you bought your first home and paid it off in order to establish the foundation for your future Findependence. Along the way you may have moved to a better home in a nicer neighbourhood and school district, which is of course the opposite of downsizing.

But at some point when it comes to housing, you may want to go in the opposite direction. A typical Victory Lap downsizing strategy is to sell the city house and rent, or sell the house and swap it for a downtown condo. Some may choose to swap one big-city home for one small urban condo *and* a vacation property. Others may do what our friends Charles and Alizun did, selling the big-city property in a hot market and moving to the country, where you can get twice the house for half the money, and put the difference into your retirement kitty.

If you were fortunate to be hired by a stable employer after college and you enrolled in the defined benefit plan (if it was on offer) then stayed put for thirty or thirty-five years, you may enjoy what many of the baby boomers' parents enjoyed: the traditional full-stop retirement as early as age fifty-five or sixty.

However, these days the job market and career paths are such that relatively few people will be able to live off a single giant stream of pension income in the end game. Odds are they will cobble together multiple pensions with smaller payouts. Some won't be real pensions in the strictest sense of the word: they will just be pots of money (defined contribution plans, IRAs, RRSPs, and the like) that need to be ultimately converted or annuitized to real pensions once you reach the stage of wanting to draw down that income. Creating new streams of income to make up for the lack of true pensions is one of the main themes of Victory Lap Retirement. It's worth noting that non-discretionary expenses all must be paid with after-tax dollars, so passive income has to be *net* of income tax.

Stage 6: Longevity & Aging

There is a final stage we'll only touch on here: longevity and aging. Clearly there are health issues to consider later in life, and thus the housing decision will expand to include things like retirement homes, assisted living, and nursing homes. There are also forms of insurance to help defray this end game of the human financial life cycle: disability insurance, critical illness insurance, and long-term care insurance being the three major ones.

Again, you may need a different kind of advice than you did during the wealth accumulation phase of your younger years. At this stage, estate planning can be crucial. For example, the death of the second spouse can often be very expensive tax-wise. You may need someone dually licensed, both to give investment advice (perhaps with a decumulation perspective) and to sell or recommend insurance products.

• • •

Aside from stages of the life cycle, you can think of the flow of money through your entire life. Early in life it will be a trickle, or even a negative outflow necessitated by taking on debt (student loans, mortgages). The challenge is to build ever-rising and multiple streams of income, so that your money is working for you, rather than the other way round. It's also worth looking at the relation between money and life energy, which we do below.

LIFE ENERGY AND FINDEPENDENCE

One of our favourite books on financial independence is *Your Money or Your Life: 9 Steps to Transforming Your Relationship with Money and Achieving Financial Independence*, by Vicki Robin and Joe Dominguez. The key concept is that of life energy and how we exchange our precious life energy for money. Many of us work hard all those years for the Corp, expending that precious life energy in exchange for a steady paycheque.

In fact, you can even consider money to be "stored life energy." Once you understand this, you become less cavalier about squandering limited financial resources on needless luxuries or wasting it in activities that don't enrich your soul. This goes to the heart of our thoughts about the benefits of frugality.

Think about how much life energy is expended to buy a luxury car. While it may be more pleasurable to drive than the average car, what if instead you bought a quality used vehicle and chose to spend the extra "found" life energy on a soul-enhancing experience, like a trip to India or returning to school to pursue a degree in theology? The precise activity will vary with the individual, of course, but hopefully you get the idea. Life energy is precious and so is money—once you view money as merely a proxy for that life energy.

When you think about money being linked to your life energy and you realize that spending money unnecessarily is also a waste of your finite life energy, it's not a good feeling, is it? This is why there is a huge literature around the so-called early retirement movement, revolving around the concept of frugality or, as we mentioned above, what we call guerrilla frugality.

Don't give in to the temptation to squander some of your precious life energy for worthless baubles, unnecessary trinkets, or things you can't afford or don't need in the first place. Or, at the very least, don't fall into debt to acquire questionable purchases.

Debt Depletes Your Life Energy in Advance

How does debt fit into this worldview, with life energy at its core? Ideally, it doesn't. We've already seen that in order to achieve Findependence, you must eliminate all debt, starting with student loans and credit cards, and ultimately even mortgage debt. Well, from the point of view of life energy, being debt-free is just as important.

How does debt differ from financial capital? Recall that in order to earn financial capital you deploy some life energy. But with debt, you haven't yet earned that financial capital, you've merely borrowed it. From whom? In effect, from your future self. You are committing your future self to expending future life energy on repaying the debt. And, of course, the price of that arrangement is interest payments. Interest rates may be low right now—they have been near historic lows for longer than either of us would have predicted—but debt is still an impediment to Findependence. And for your life energy, it's simply crushing.

It's easy to see why debt is so alluring on the surface. Instead of working first and then receiving financial capital, with debt you first receive the financial capital, *then* you slowly pay off the loan by committing some of your future time and life energy. You are essentially putting the cart before the horse. And you are sentencing yourself to working and spending your valuable life energy to repay the financial capital you have already borrowed and used. How demoralizing is that?

Have you noticed that despite "near-zero" interest rates when you're a creditor (that is, when you invest in low-paying bonds, GICs, or CDs—more on these later, see page 78), your investment return is tiny; but when the shoe is on the other foot and you're a debtor, suddenly interest rates are gigantic? Anyone with credit-card debt close to 20 per cent per annum (after tax) knows this well, and the same goes for anyone who finds themselves in arrears to tax authorities. Penalties and compounding interest soon become huge impediments to your potential financial freedom. You are virtually "shackled" by such debts. No matter what stage of the financial life cycle you are in, make breaking free from the chains of debt your first priority. Not only will debt limit your financial freedom severely, it will suck the life right out of you.

Don't Confuse Needs and Wants

Advertising is the art of convincing people to spend money they don't have on things they don't need.
—*Will Rogers*

Preserving life energy and being frugal with money can be a liberating concept, but unfortunately capitalist society conspires against this. In order to keep growing the economy and to make money for themselves, makers of goods and suppliers of services are engaged in a never-ending battle to separate you from your hard-earned money and, hence, the life energy expended to earn that financial capital in the first place. Marketers are constantly trying to sell us "stuff" or "experiences" whether we need them or not. The main message is that in order to achieve happiness and have the ideal life we dream about, we need to keep buying more stuff. And stuff, of course, costs money.

Ed's ball got a lot larger after he
bought the bigger house in the suburbs...

The average child watches an astounding total of 20,000 thir-
ty-second commercials per year. Adults are no better: they
spend at least three years of their lives watching commercials.
There seems to be a constant battle going on in our minds between what we have, what we need, and what advertisers tell us
we should want. Many financial problems could be alleviated
if people spent the time distinguishing between a "need" and
a "want" prior to buying something. But because of an ever-
expanding definition of need, things once considered luxuries
have somehow become necessities.

A good example is the modern "monster" home. In Mike's
case, his family needed a roof over its head, but did he have to
buy a 3,000-square-foot castle like he did? He was raised in a
1,250-square-foot home with a similar-sized family and it seemed
to do the job quite nicely. Think about it in terms of the mortgage: if he had bought a smaller house, his mortgage would have
been much smaller and cheaper to service. Had that been the

case, Mike's financial independence (i.e., his Findependence Day) would have arrived that much sooner.

So when you look at your current mortgage, you need to view it as part need, with the balance of it being a want. When you finally start to realize the number of "needs" you purchase compared to the "wants," you start to see the world a little differently. There is no doubt that we are all being played by marketers and advertisers, but the good news is that once you accept that more stuff does not equate to more happiness, you can break the spell and begin to build an immunity against advertising. Once you reach this point, you will begin to see advertisements in a different light and laugh at their attempts to seduce you.

A FORMULA FOR FREEDOM

Both of us wish we had been taught the lessons of Findependence before starting our careers. When you understand why something is so important, it's much easier to attain it! So it is our hope that, now that you know how important a goal financial freedom is, you will be motivated to adopt a more frugal lifestyle and to save in a disciplined way during your full-time working years. Over that time, through a combination of expense cutting and increases in active income, you will eventually be able to generate enough passive income to cover your cost of living: that's the Holy Grail of Findependence. And don't forget to have a big party once you reach your Findependence Day! That's what Jonathan did when he turned sixty in early 2013. It was the world's first *Findependence Day* celebration!

To recap, your Findependence Day is the day all your sources of passive income exceed your non-discretionary expenses. Findependence is a powerful concept and the main takeaway is

best described in the following formula, which we introduced at
the start of this chapter:

PASSIVE INCOME > NON-DISCRETIONARY EXPENSES = FREEDOM

The day this formula holds true for you is the day you can finally
stop working for money just to meet your basic survival expenses.
You can still earn extra income for special trips and luxuries, but
you no longer have to worry about how you'll meet the rent in-
stalment or mortgage payment. If you've read this far, you know
that we don't advocate having a mortgage once you reach the
stage people have traditionally called "retirement." In fact, we'd
go so far as to say that if you're not financially independent, you
have no business even fantasizing about retirement. Conversely,
it's possible to be financially independent but *not* retired; indeed
that's one of the key concepts in Victory Lap. This book's authors
are in this camp.

ENJOY YOUR FREEDOM: YOU'VE EARNED IT!

Worry often gives a small thing a big shadow.
— *Swedish proverb*

When you achieve Findependence, or financial freedom, you
have freed yourself from fear about money. Don't sit there and
waste time worrying about how long you will live, how the government is squeezing you, or how the world has gone mad. Ignore
the noise and spend your time and money doing things you enjoy
while there is still time to do them. Remember, no one gives you
a prize (except perhaps your beneficiaries) for being the richest
person in the graveyard.

Back in chapter 1 we described what is a common reality of retirement for many: we portrayed a grey-haired couple living in a small bungalow, spending most of their day watching television, splurging a couple of times a month for dinner at Swiss Chalet. This is what life is like for people who live hovering near the Findependence threshold.

Chapter 5 is for people who don't want to spend what time they have left on a couch watching the world go by. They want much more, and the creation of a Victory Lap lifestyle gives it to them. But before we get to that, chapter 4 reviews the seven eternal truths of financial independence.

4

The Seven Eternal Truths of Financial Independence

Doctors know needles hurt. They give shots nonetheless. Why? Because they know that little bit of discomfort up front leads to miracles down the road.
—*Don Connelly*

You must gain control over your money or the lack of it will forever control you.
—*Dave Ramsey*

In the previous chapter, we looked at the importance of financial independence and how it's a prerequisite to the new stage of life we call Victory Lap Retirement. We also looked at the average human's financial life cycle, which starts roughly at age twenty and extends well into old age. We did this because, as with the human life cycle itself, most of us go through predictable stages of our financial lives.

We all start out our financial lives with zero financial capital (unless you were fortunate enough to inherit) but with millions

And Jonathan descended from the mountain with the 7 Truths for Financial Freedom.

of dollars of potential earning capacity, or human capital. The objective is to spend your so-called "working years" gradually converting that human capital into financial capital, because one day you won't be able to earn income anymore.

The financial life cycle is important, but it takes a chronological approach to life. We described the need for reducing debt and being frugal, behaviour which once you're debt-free can then be used to build wealth and ultimately attain Findependence.

Once you've achieved the ultimate goal of financial freedom, you can take the traditional "full-stop" retirement, as many dream of, or embark on your Victory Lap. You may choose a brand new career, launch a new business, or merely work part-time to supplement multiple streams of income. Or you might create a "portfolio career," dabbling in various hobbies that may or may not pay; or retrain, or go back to school in the hopes of turning something you love into a gig that will supplement those income sources.

In the pages that follow in this chapter, instead of looking at Findependence through a chronological lens, we go into more depth about seven "eternal truths" about money. You could call them the basic truths about personal finance in general, but they apply equally to Findependence. In fact, this chapter originally appeared as seven columns by Jonathan in the *Financial Post*, which ran in the summer of 2015. We are grateful to the *Post* for allowing us to publish them in a new (and revised) format for this book.

The original idea was sparked by a confession made by one of the most experienced personal finance writers in North America, the *Wall Street Journal*'s Jason Zweig. After writing his 250th "Intelligent Investor" column, Zweig admitted in print that there are only a handful of personal finance stories out there:

> *I was once asked, at a journalism conference, how I defined my job. I said: My job is to write the exact same thing between fifty and 100 times a year in such a way that neither my editors nor my readers will ever think I am repeating myself. That's because good advice rarely changes, while markets change constantly.*

As a long-time personal finance columnist, Zweig's admission resonated with Jonathan, and he started to think about what these "core" stories that keep recurring might be. As you'll soon see, many of the seven truths we go on to discuss here dovetail nicely with the frugality theme we explored in the previous chapter. Live by them and you will naturally get closer to your goal of Findependence.

ETERNAL TRUTH #1: LIVE BELOW YOUR MEANS

This is the granddaddy principle of financial independence. Without it, there's little point talking about the rest. The only way to become financially independent is to be consistent about spending less than you earn, year in and year out, decade in and decade out. The attitude required is the one described in the previous chapter—guerrilla frugality.

Consider first the antithesis of financial independence: being heavily in debt. How does this sad state of affairs arise in the first place? By living beyond one's means: spending one's fool head off to the point where frivolous expenditures and the interest on your debt exceed what's coming in. This is a recipe for disaster, and bankruptcy courts are testament to the inevitable fate of those who fail to live within their means.

As we are writing about eternal verities here, we'll resort to a much-used (and especially apt) quotation about the formula for happiness, which is attributed to Charles Dickens. In *David Copperfield* the character Micawber famously says, "Annual income twenty pounds, annual expenditure nineteen [pounds] nineteen [shillings] and six [pence], result happiness. Annual income twenty pounds, annual expenditure twenty pounds ought and six, result misery." Translated into twenty-first century American or Canadian, this might read, "Annual income $50,000, annual expenses $40,000, result happiness. Annual income $50,000, annual expenses $60,000, result misery."

In the latter part of either quote, we see the unhappy result of living beyond one's means. If your expenditures are even slightly higher than your income, you are by definition falling gradually into debt. If this takes the form of non–tax-deductible credit-card consumer debt, odds are you'll be paying something like 20 per cent interest annually. To pay that off, you'd have to generate investment returns of about 40 per cent before tax if you're in the top tax bracket. No reliable investments can give you that kind of return, unless perhaps you were shrewd enough to buy into the Visa initial public offering several years ago. (Clearly it's better to be on the *receiving* end of the interest on debt, not on the "dishing it out" end.)

It is far better to live within your means, as in the first part of Micawber's formula for happiness. If you earn more than you spend, there is a surplus, which becomes the basis for "savings." Most personal finance and investing lore is all about how to make those savings go the furthest. With interest rates so low and interest income taxed at the highest rates (relative to capital gains and dividends), you need to invest those savings into vehicles that offer a better chance at long-term growth. Most often, that's going to be stocks (also known as equities), as well as equity exchange-traded funds and equity mutual funds.

The difference between what you (and your spouse, if applicable) earn and what you spend becomes your capital. Capital is precious and should never be squandered. Most of us must generate capital with after-tax earnings, but if you acquire some capital in an easier manner—inheritance, lottery wins, severance packages—it's still precious. You never want to "break into capital." If you're already accustomed to living within your means, you'll try to spend only the interest and dividends generated by that capital. To do that, the capital must be invested wisely and in a tax-efficient manner. We'll look again at "decumulation" and related issues later in the book.

ETERNAL TRUTH #2: PAY YOURSELF FIRST

The second eternal truth of financial independence is closely related to living below your means. The principle of "paying yourself first" has been enshrined in every major personal finance book since 1926, when George Samuel Clason's *The Richest Man in Babylon* was published. It's the single-most powerful message in David Chilton's best-seller, *The Wealthy Barber*, and has been incorporated into several books by David Bach, all bearing in part the phrase *The Automatic Millionaire*.

Clason started it all by writing a series of pamphlets for banks and insurance companies about thrift and financial success in the 1920s. These were later gathered together to become the book, ostensibly a collection of parables set in ancient Babylon. The richest man in those parables is Arkad, who when entreated by his friends to reveal the secret of his wealth, said he discovered it once he had decided that "a part of all I earned was mine to keep." When the friends naively asked whether they did not already keep all that they earned, Arkad replied in the negative, pointing out that much of what they earned had to go to things like food and clothing.

These days, of course, a good chunk of our paycheque goes to taxes, housing, energy, transportation, and so on; we are all well aware of the multiple demands on our purse. The key is to *pay yourself first* by putting aside at least 10 per cent into savings the moment you receive your paycheque or any other money. Arkad told his acolytes that regularly saving at least one-tenth of their income (or better yet, more, if they could afford to) and putting that money to work earning interest, they would eventually become wealthy.

David Chilton's mega–best-seller, first published in 1989, also advocated paying yourself first; however, because modern interest income generates hardly any return and is taxed harshly, Chilton's spin was to "be an owner, not a loaner," meaning that 10 per cent savings would have a better shot at long-term growth by being invested in stocks instead of cash or bonds. When his book was published, Chilton said equity mutual funds were a good way to diversify stock holdings. This message was gratefully received by the mutual fund industry, which bought multiple copies of the book. His follow-up, *The Wealthy Barber Returns*, is less effusive about mutual funds; like many cost-conscious personal finance gurus these days, Chilton likes exchange-traded funds or ETFs.

David Bach's books in *The Automatic Millionaire* series took these concepts and emphasized that the best way to pay yourself first was to automate the process by arranging things so that the 10 per cent was taken from your paycheque right off the top through an "automatic draft" (as it's called in the U.S.) that takes the money as soon as you're paid by your employer and transfers it to your financial institution to be invested. In Canada, an automatic draft is usually referred to as a "pre-authorized chequing" arrangement, or PAC.

The effect is similar to what happens when income tax is deducted from your paycheque "at source." It's gone before you can spend it and, therefore, you don't really miss it. Yes, you may feel a bit "broke" after the double whammy of paying tribute to the taxman as well as paying yourself first, but as the years go by and your wealth steadily mounts, you'll be glad you embraced this particular truth.

We said above that "pay yourself first" is closely tied to the first eternal truth of "live within your means." The reason should be obvious. The only way you can save 10 per cent or more of your paycheque is if you are spending less than you are bringing in. If you're earning $50,000 a year and spending $50,000 a year, there is no surplus and, therefore, no way to pay yourself first. And no, using your credit cards to buy investments is definitely not the way to go.

It follows that you need to be frugal enough that you have a surplus between what you earn and what you spend. As Arkad pointed out, if you're not careful, you'll be paying everyone else ahead of yourself. So exercise guerrilla frugality, set up a PAC, and invest the savings wisely. How do you do this? Well, before we tackle that subject we must first look at our third eternal truth: debt.

ETERNAL TRUTH #3: GET OUT OF DEBT

The financial media spill a lot of ink and spend a lot of airtime on investing, perhaps because following the latest hot stock can be a fascinating pastime for those so inclined. Who among us isn't interested in what Apple is doing, or Google, Facebook, or recent new arrivals like Shopify?

But if you're young and still in debt—whether because of student loans, credit cards, mortgages, or car loans—you really shouldn't be fretting about investing in stocks, equity funds, or even "safe" fixed-income vehicles like guaranteed investment certificates (GICs) or certificates of deposit (CDs), which are the U.S. version of GICs. What's the point of owning a stock that pays a 3 per cent annual dividend, or a CD paying 1 per cent or 2 per cent per annum, when your credit-card debt is costing you 18 per cent a year?

It's a fact that no investment you own—even if it's held in a U.S. Roth IRA (Individual Retirement Arrangement) or a Canadian Tax-Free Savings Account (TFSA)—is going to outperform the simple act of paying off high-interest, non–tax-deductible consumer debt. In fact, if you're in the top tax bracket, you'd have to generate about a 40 per cent annual return pre-tax just to pay off 20 per cent annual credit-card debt after taxes.

Credit cards are one of the most probable causes of consumer debt that leads to bankruptcy. Even though interest rates have been hovering near record lows since the financial crisis hit in 2008, it's a sad fact that credit-card interest charges have remained stubbornly high. Speaking from Jonathan's own youthful experience, the trap of paying off only the minimum monthly payment is an easy one to fall into. That's what the credit-card companies would love you to do, but it's almost the worst practice to engage in for anyone who cares about their personal finances. Pay off the entire balance in full each month and make a solemn pledge to yourself that you'll never pay a dime in credit-card interest.

While student loans tend to levy far lower punitive rates of interest, these, too, can cause trouble if they are neglected and you start to let negative compound interest eat away at your net worth. In fact, in September 2015, a report from the U.S. Government Accountability Office (GAO) found that many seniors at or near retirement still owe money from student loans taken out decades earlier. As a result, some are being forced to pay by having a portion of their Social Security cheques garnisheed at source.

Another common source of trouble is falling behind on tax payments to the Internal Revenue Service (IRS) or the Canada Revenue Agency (CRA). A combination of late-filing penalties and compound interest on the debt can create liabilities that eventually grow bigger than, and in addition to, the amounts initially outstanding. So even though we would suggest that those who are solvent should invest as much as possible in IRAs, Roth plans, RRSPs, and TFSAs, this may not hold for those at any age who have significant debts, whether consumer debt or money owing to the taxman.

The one debt we'd tolerate is mortgage debt, as for most young people, taking out a mortgage is the only way to get a first step on the housing ladder, and mortgage rates are much more reasonable than what credit-card companies charge. Having said that, at today's high home prices, this is a significant undertaking and so we recommend striving to come up with a full 20 per cent for the down payment (perhaps financed through savings in a Roth or TFSA), then aim to pay the mortgage off within five or ten years. Difficult if you're a sole breadwinner but certainly doable if you're one-half of a dual-income couple.

The nice thing is that the frugal behaviour that is required to pay down a mortgage can be continued once the debt is retired;

at that point, if you continue to be disciplined and live well below your means (remember Truth #1!), that same behaviour can be used to start building up wealth, if you save and invest the money that used to go toward paying off the mortgage.

If you're well along the road to owning your home out-right—we still say a paid-for home is the foundation of financial independence (see Truth #4)—you should try to avoid using that home equity to access more cash. During the financial crisis, the temptation to view home equity as a sort of ATM made things worse for many homeowners. We would avoid home equity lines of credit (HELOCs) except in cases of dire emergency, such as job loss. And while reverse mortgages appear to be on the rise, we view taking on a reverse mortgage in old age as being unadvisable except for very specialized cases.

In short, you should retire all debt before retiring yourself!

ETERNAL TRUTH #4: BUY A HOME AND PAY IT OFF AS SOON AS POSSIBLE

We've always said that a paid-for home is the foundation of finan-cial independence. You have to live somewhere, and you can't live in an IRA or an RRSP. Most of us have a simple choice: either become a homeowner or rent from someone who is a homeowner. You may rationalize when you're young that you don't want to be tied down to a mortgage. But consider that when you're renting, you are still paying a mortgage—your landlord's!

The problem with being a perpetual tenant is that the rent will never stop and your landlord will likely hike the rent in line with inflation. When you own your own home, the total outlay may exceed your rent in the first few years; but eventually, as you pay down principal, more and more of each mortgage payment will be used to pay down still more principal, and less interest relative to principal. Tie this in with taking advantage of the annual prepayment privileges—generally 10 to 15 per cent of initial principal—and there will come a day when your mortgage is fully paid off. On that fine day, you'll no longer be paying interest or principal and you will own your home free and clear. For the rest of your days, you'll be able to live rent-free!

Let's say that it took a person ten years to pay off her mortgage. Compare this to the situation she'd be in if she had continued to rent all that time. In year eleven, she'd still be renting and likely shelling out a good deal more per month than when she first signed her lease. And unlike the mortgage, there would be no prospect of those rent payments ever ceasing. But a homeowner who pays off the mortgage after ten years will forevermore be living essentially rent-free, although of course there will still be property taxes, utility bills, and perhaps maintenance fees if the home is a condo.

We don't know about you, but we'd far rather enter retirement or semi-retirement with no mortgage, or with any other debt for that matter. Not having to come up with the monthly rent means your monthly "nut" is that much lower. You won't have to earn as much and so you will also pay less income tax.

There are several more benefits to having a paid-off home:

- First, a principal residence is a major form of tax shelter, right up there with owning your own business. This is because Ottawa does not tax any capital gains on your primary home. (The rules are more nuanced in the United States.) If you bought for $400,000 and years later sold for $800,000, you'd have a tax-free capital gain of $400,000 that could be added to the rest of your retirement nest egg.

- Second, if you have a good chunk of equity in your home, it can be used as collateral for an emergency source of cash. You could access a home equity line of credit that, though we strongly advise against it, could be used to renovate the home, put on an addition, or go on a major vacation. Similarly, retirees with no heirs who find themselves house-rich but cash-poor could always resort to a reverse mortgage to convert some of the home's equity to a tax-free source of cash. Again, we wouldn't recommend this for most people and perhaps especially not if your children or other heirs view such an act as potentially cutting into their inheritance. But in certain situations this may be an option for those who really want to stay put and who have few, if any, alternative sources of retirement income.

- A third possibility, which is really a variation of tapping your home's equity, is downsizing at some point. A typical retirement fantasy is to sell the suburban monster home and swap it for a downtown condo *and* a cottage on a lake somewhere or a winter home in warmer climes. Assuming that the condo and cottage are each roughly half the price of the big home being sold, you'd essentially be swapping one home for two. Because of the capital gains exemption on the principal residence, there would be no tax consequences on selling it, although normal real estate brokerage commissions and land transfer taxes would have to be considered. Alternatively, you could sell the big-city home for a similarly large home in the country, perhaps getting twice the house for half the money and adding the difference to your retirement kitty.

To us, nothing beats the security of having a paid-for home. It lowers your expenses (your "monthly nut") and increases your options and flexibility, which is why we view it as the foundation of financial independence.

ETERNAL TRUTH #5: BE AN OWNER, NOT A LOANER

Savings is, by general definition, the difference between the amount of money you earn and the amount you spend. As we've seen, to create a surplus, obviously you must spend less than you earn. If there's a deficit and you spend more than you make, you have the problem of debt, which we addressed in Truth #3. But even if you live frugally within your means and pay yourself first, you're not going to get rich just leaving your savings in a bank account that pays almost zero interest.

Since the financial crisis hit in 2008, interest rates have hovered near generational lows, and the after-tax pittance that's paid in bank accounts—or even in CDs (in the U.S.), GICs (in Canada), or money-market mutual funds anywhere—is unlikely even to match the rate of inflation. If inflation is running at 2 per cent a year and you're receiving 1 per cent in interest, you're not even treading water, you're losing money. The "real" (that is, after-inflation) return in this case is minus 1 per cent. Even worse, what little interest you are being paid will be taxed at your highest marginal rate, just like the last dollar you earn on your salary, or any bonuses.

Rather than loaning your money out through bonds, GICs, savings bonds, and the like, you need to embrace the concept of being an owner rather than a loaner. In practice, being an owner means owning stocks of quality businesses or equity mutual funds or equity exchange-traded funds that provide exposure to a whole basket of such enterprises. Of course, you can also start your own business and be the owner of a bricks-and-mortar enterprise or one based on the Web. But for the purposes of this book, we'll assume you're taking the diversified ownership route of investing in equities.

A basic axiom of investing (it could even be our eighth Truth!) is that risk and return are related. Being a loaner supposedly entails low risk, so the expected return is low. Being an owner of a business or of equities entails more risk, so the expected return should be higher.

One route to mitigate risk somewhat would be to focus on quality dividend-paying stocks. These days you can find utilities, banks, pharmaceutical, and telecommunications stocks paying dividends anywhere between 3 and 5 per cent, which is a far sight better than the 1 per cent you might get from loaning your money out. Stocks also address two big long-term risks facing retirees: inflation and longevity. Over time, you can expect dividend hikes that keep pace with or beat inflation, plus growth of the underlying capital.

The bonus is that this higher dividend income is taxed more preferentially than the interest income that goes to loaners. In both the United States and Canada, dividends from qualifying corporations are taxed much less harshly than interest income, thus providing a return roughly double that of interest income and on an after-tax basis, as much as triple. Of course, this applies primarily to taxable or "non-registered" investment accounts.

The other benefit of being an owner rather than a loaner is capital gains. When you're an owner, you can win twice: once on the dividend (if any) and again if the stock rises in value over the time you own it. For starters, only half your capital gains (in Canada) are taxed (it's called the 50 per cent inclusion rate), so you should be able to keep roughly three-quarters of the return from the capital gains. Additionally, you can avoid even the partial tax as long as you buy and hold the stock without taking profits and "crystallizing" the gain. And lastly, even if you do choose to take partial profits, you may be able to neutralize the tax consequences by selling an equal amount of another stock on which you've suffered capital losses. The rules are a bit more complex in the United States, where capital gains taxes are more severe if you trade frequently.

Capital losses, you say? Yes, Virginia, the downside of all this ownership potential is that you must be prepared for an investment in any given stock to lose value from time to time. Capital gains and even steady dividends are not guaranteed the way a CD or GIC "guarantees" an annual payout of 1 per cent or 2 per cent (guaranteed to lose to inflation, we'd say!).

You'll want to work with a financial adviser to determine an appropriate mix of stocks and debt instruments, depending on how much risk and volatility you can stomach. This investment mix is called a balanced portfolio, and the asset allocation (a fancy way of describing the mix and proportion of different kinds of investments you hold) will tell you how much you should be an owner and how much a loaner.

ETERNAL TRUTH #6: NEVER SAY NO TO FREE MONEY FROM YOUR EMPLOYER

As a general principal, we're wary of any scheme that promises something for nothing. Blindly entering such transactions is a good way to get scammed. However, when it's your employer offering you free money, we think it's safe to say you should take them up on any such offers. If your boss gave you a big raise or an annual bonus, you wouldn't say no, would you? For the

same reason, you shouldn't say no to one of the best freebies that
employers can offer: membership in the company pension plan.
This is an especially good deal if your employer still offers an
old-fashioned defined benefit pension or if they "match" your
contributions for group 401(k) employer pensions offered in the
United States or the equivalent defined-contribution pension
plans in Canada.

The beauty of company pension plans is that they take advantage of some of our earlier eternal truths. If your contributions
are taken right off your paycheques at source as is done with income tax, then you'll hardly miss what you never saw. Such an
automatic savings plan simultaneously forces you to live within
your means and pay yourself first, and over time it takes advantage of tax-free compounding. And remember, just as it is the
case with personal lump-sum contributions to IRAs or RRSPs,
regular payments into a pension plan should be accompanied by
slightly less tax deducted at source: in effect, you get your tax re-
fund with every paycheque. If this doesn't happen automatically,
ask your Human Resources department to help; you may have to
sign a form informing the tax department of this arrangement.

Another big source of corporate free money is discounted
stock, assuming that your employer is a big, publicly traded company. Here again, you can arrange to have some of each paycheque
directed to the stock purchase plan, yet another way you can pay
yourself first. A typical arrangement is a 20 per cent discount the
first year, a 30 per cent discount the second year, and 50 per cent
thereafter. If the stock in question also pays a dividend, that will
be a welcome source of investment income down the road, and
you don't have to pay a commission to buy company stock.

What we like about such arrangements is the built-in "margin of safety" that value investors often talk about. You're getting
a price that the general public cannot get, so even if the stock

does not appreciate in price, once you're free to sell (a specific number of months may be required before you're permitted to sell a portion of your holdings), you really have an instant profit. For example, say your company stock trades at $100 a share on the open market but you received a 30 per cent discount. That means it cost you just $70 for something that's worth $100. If you sell on the open market, you will receive $100, less brokerage commissions, for a quick $30 profit. That's free money!

Be mindful, however, that the taxman will be your silent partner. With this in mind, we'd advise you to let your stake build over time and to reinvest the dividends in still more shares. Unfortunately, the tax collector will probably view the discount as a taxable benefit, and if you do sell at a profit you will also have to pay capital gains taxes when it comes time to file your annual income taxes.

For building wealth through the company you work for, it's hard to beat joining the pension plan and taking them up on the stock purchase plan. But don't forget the smaller freebies that may also be on offer. Subsidized cafeterias or free coffee or soft drinks can add up to substantial savings over time, as can subsidized corporate gyms if they're on offer. The latter is a great, almost-free perk, and consider the health benefits of exercising while you're still at work. You might even rationalize, "Hey, they're paying me to exercise," even if your workout occurs during your lunch break.

Still another source of corporate free money is discounts on whatever products or services your company is in the business of providing to the public. Jonathan's last corporate job had, in addition to everything discussed above, half-price employee offers on cable TV, Internet service, and magazine subscriptions. These days we're all so connected to our various devices, you don't need us to remind you of the great savings made possible by these deals.

Finally, while it may not be clear that there are savings and discounts involved, you should investigate the value of the company medical, dental, drug, and insurance plans. Even if you have to pay for some of these through deductions on your paycheque, there may be some matching by your employer. If you need some or all of these plans anyway, what your employer offers could well be a better deal than what you'd be able to obtain on the open market, although you'd be wise to shop around or consult an insurance agent or benefits consultant before blindly signing up to everything.

Your HR department can provide an annual summary of the true value of your employment contract, above and beyond the basic salary. Your general attitude to any offers of free money should be, "I'm in!"

ETERNAL TRUTH #7: TAKE THE GOVERNMENT UP ON ITS FEW OFFERS OF FREE MONEY

The seventh and final eternal truth of financial independence is to accept all offers of free money from the government. Superficially, this resembles our sixth truth, to accept all freebies offered by your employer; however, when the government is involved (whether it be Washington or Ottawa), opportunities for free money are few and far between.

Yes, if you're among society's most disadvantaged, the government may actually redistribute enough money from the wealthy to the poor that this would constitute "free money" for the recipients involved. But most readers of this book will be paying a lot more in taxes on salaries, investments, and consumption than they will be receiving on a net basis. Either way, the general principle still holds: even if it's just a question of minimizing the tax haul for the federal government and its counterparts in the states or provinces, a tax break is still a version of free money.

A good example of this in the United States is that citizens are able to deduct the interest expense on their home mortgages, a tax break that is not available north of the border. However, Canadians get a different kind of tax freebie with the capital gains tax exemption on principal residences. Again, this is not so much a gift as it is a lower-than-usual form of punishment by taxation. But relative to most taxes, it's a break that's right up there with business ownership.

Social Security in the United States and, in Canada, the triad of the Canada Pension Plan, Old Age Security, and Guaranteed Income Supplement are the most obvious examples of "free" money coming from government, even if they are, in effect, a return of contributions paid out over your working years.

This brings us to ways of sheltering or at least deferring tax on investments—now we're definitely in the realm of minimizing taxation, not of actually getting a net benefit from government. Both countries offer tax incentives to build up retirement savings: the more you contribute to an Individual Retirement Account (IRA) in the U.S., or a Registered Retirement Savings Plan (RRSP) in Canada, the lower your taxable income.

IRAs and RRSPs have two big tax benefits: First, they give you an upfront tax deduction, which you can generate by making a contribution in the previous tax year and then filing your taxes on time. This especially benefits those in higher tax brackets, as the contribution immediately lowers your taxable income. The second benefit is ongoing sheltering of investment income that would otherwise generate annual tax on interest, dividend income, and possibly capital gains.

Both countries also have other mirror-image tax sheltering programs, Roth IRAs in the United States and their Canadian

equivalent: Tax-Free Savings Accounts (TFSAs). Neither Roths
nor TFSAs offer the upfront tax deductions on offer from IRAs
or RRSPs; but on the other hand, later in life Roths and TFSAs
will allow you to draw income tax-free. That's the kind of thing
we mean by not saying no to government freebies from Uncle
Sam or Ottawa.

Like many other government freebies, RRSPs and IRAs are
not outright gifts. The hitch is that one day when you want to
withdraw the funds, you'll be taxed at your top marginal rate
on forced annual withdrawals in old age, as well as on voluntary
withdrawals at any age. However, the tax-free compounding
you'll enjoy for many years is certainly better than being fully
taxed each year on investments that are not sheltered by these
government-sponsored vehicles. And if you wind up in a lower
tax bracket in retirement than you were when you were working,
the difference in tax rates could be considered a type of government "gift."

There are, of course, scores of other supposed freebies in the
tax statutes of both countries, which is one reason tax codes are
so complex and infuriating.

• • •

There is nothing magical about the number seven, but we'd wa-
ger that anyone who takes this list of eternal truths to heart and
actually incorporates them into their daily lives will be well on
the way to financial independence. And just for fun, when you
read articles on personal finance in the daily press, try to see
whether they are a version of one of our seven truths. You may
be surprised how often these basic principles keep turning up
in different guises. Most of the seven truths will help you reach
Findependence earlier than if you didn't practice them, but almost all of them also apply once you've begun your Victory Lap.

MAPPING THE ETERNAL TRUTHS TO THE LIFE CYCLE

Now that you've read this chapter, you may want to go back to chapter 3 and revisit the financial life cycle. The first few eternal truths (Live Below Your Means, Pay Yourself First) map directly to the early stages of the financial life cycle (Debt and Frugality, Family Formation and Housing). Some of the investment-oriented truths map to Building Wealth, and the last few on never saying no to employers' or government money can be mapped to the latter stages of the life cycle you'll encounter during your Victory Lap, particularly the Decumulation and Downsizing stage.

It's not a one-to-one mapping exercise, however: A life cycle is a linear progression from youth to old age, whereas the eternal truths of financial independence can be used wherever you may be in the financial life cycle. For example, we think that living within your means is something best practiced throughout the whole life cycle; frugality gets you out of debt and is the basis for building wealth, which, if kept up long enough, eventually gets you to Findependence. And once you've achieved Findependence, it sets you up for Victory Lap Retirement.

So let's assume you've absorbed the seven truths and that they've allowed you to reach Findependence. Now—finally!—we're ready to get into some depth about how to establish your own personal Victory Lap. See you in chapter 5!

5

Victory Lap Retirement

A master in the art of living draws no sharp distinction between his work and his play, his labor and his leisure, his mind and his body, his education and his recreation. He hardly knows which is which. He simply pursues his vision of excellence through whatever he is doing and leaves others to determine whether he is working or playing. To him, he is always doing both.
—*Lawrence Pearsall Jacks*

LESSONS FROM OKINAWA

Okinawa is a chain of islands off the coast of Japan and is home to some of the healthiest seniors on the planet, with many living past the century mark. Not only are these seniors among the longest-lived in the world, they also benefit from more healthy years, free from disability and illness. Heart disease and dementia rates are lower than average, and rates for breast and prostate cancer are even lower still. Obviously the elders of Okinawa are doing something right! Being smart people, why

wouldn't we try to copy what they are doing? It would only seem to make sense, right?

In chapter 1 we described how in North America the concept of retirement evolved during the industrialization of the continent. Prior to that, most people lived on farms and farmers didn't retire. This is very similar to the thinking among Okinawan people, who refuse to believe in the concept of retirement and do not practice it. It's interesting to note that in the Okinawan language there isn't even a word for retirement. In its place is the term *ikigai* (eek-y-guy), which roughly translated means, "the reason for which you wake up in the morning."

Ikigai really means having a sense of purpose. There is a great deal of literature supporting the idea that people who have a strong sense of purpose are healthier and better able to deal with the difficulties that life may occasionally throw their way. Older Okinawans can readily articulate the reason why they get up in the morning. They live intentional, purposeful lives. They feel needed, they matter, they contribute, and as a result they live longer than most.

Once you have found your *ikigai*, why would you ever want to retire? What would you wish to retire to? People need a reason to live, and continuing to work at something they find enjoyable gives them that reason. Why would they ever want to take it away from themselves via retirement?

VICTORY LAP LIFESTYLE

In his book *The Blue Zones: Lessons for Living Longer from the People Who've Lived the Longest*, Dan Buettner clearly demonstrates how lifestyle choices are the key to a healthy and active old age. This is evidenced by the younger people of Okinawa who are seduced by the lure of high-paying jobs in high-stress environments, have poor diets, and don't get enough exercise. As a result, they are succumbing to the illnesses (heart disease, stroke, cancer, etc.) that the elders have managed to avoid. The younger people want more and they want it now, but the chase for more is killing them.

This kind of mentality is more in keeping with another Japanese word, one that is decidedly more ominous: *karoshi*, which means "death from overwork," caused by a lack of work–life balance. Sounds like we might be suffering from a little *karoshi* here in North America as well—working flat out for decades to attain the dream of a full-stop retirement that we may never live to see. Do you think maybe we have got this retirement thing all wrong? We sure think so.

After reviewing much of the prevailing retirement literature and longevity studies, we have concluded that for most of us a full-stop retirement is not the best way to go. People need to stop spending so much time worrying about making more money and worrying about retirement. Instead we should be focusing our efforts on making a great life while we still have the time. We need to work on optimizing our lifestyle with the goal of maximizing our life expectancy and the overall quality of our remaining years. We hate to break it to you, but sitting on a beach all day drinking piña coladas just isn't going to do it for you after a week or two.

In fact, a study published in 2005 that looked at Shell Oil employees in the United States showed that people who retired at age fifty-five were 89 per cent more likely to die in the ten years after retirement than those who retired at sixty-five. The same study found that the workers who continued working to the age of sixty-five were 89 per cent more likely to live ten more years after retirement even though they were ten years older than their early-retirement counterparts.

These findings suggest that, without a purpose, without a reason to get out of bed in the morning, people tend to live shorter lives. For many of us, work is our purpose and so when we retire we are in fact retiring from our purpose. Without purpose, we do not have a good reason to live, which is a sad way to go through the rest of your life. It's also important to note that just because you have achieved financial independence, it does not automatically mean that you will be living a fulfilling life. A life without purpose even if you have a lot of money is a sad life indeed.

The aforementioned Shell Oil employees and the elders in Okinawa are just a few examples of numerous longevity studies that have had similar findings, and the lessons they teach us are reflected in the new lifestyle philosophy of Victory Lap. The goal in Victory Lap is a re-balancing of leisure and work in a person's life in order to create a vibrant, healthy, low-stress, sustainable lifestyle.

The key is to slow down the pace of your life, even in the working years (which in turn will lower stress and anxiety), and to stay engaged and active later in life than the traditional full-stop retirement might allow. As we say in the subtitle of this book, we all need to learn to play a little more while we are working, and continue working to some degree while we are playing. This re-distribution of work and leisure is a true work–life balance and is much healthier all around than the old slave-and-save retirement model. As we have seen, what makes this ideal balance attainable and sustainable is first achieving Findependence.

We all must stop spending so much time chasing the big ex-pensive pleasures in life; instead, we need to learn to enjoy the many little pleasures we often miss when we're wrapped up in our busy business lives. By slowing down you begin to see and appreciate things as if for the first time. You begin to live a more fulfilled life because you finally realize you are satisfied with where you are—you don't need to keep chasing more. Or as re-tirement expert Doug Dahmer puts it, you've reached the "Work Optional" stage. You finally understand that you have enough money to get by and that there are other, far better, reasons to get out of bed in the morning.

START PLANNING YOUR VICTORY LAP NOW

Smart Victory Lappers plan their exit from the corporate world well in advance. They view their corporate jobs as stepping stones toward the time when they won't have to worry about impressing the boss anymore and they will no longer have to endure time-sucking commutes, job plateauing, office politics, endless meetings, and pressured sales just for the money. And when they get to that point of financial independence, they don't wait for permission from someone to say it's okay for them to leave their primary job to start their Victory Lap: it was their plan all along.

By thinking this way and planning ahead, you will have a second chance in Victory Lap, and this time you'll get to connect the dots your way. Realize that most of your major responsibilities are now behind you, such as raising and educating the kids, paying down the mortgage, and achieving Findependence. No matter what happens, you and your family will survive. So stop putting things off till tomorrow, because tomorrow you could be suffering from a life-changing illness. Never assume that opportunities that are available to you today will be available to you five years from now. Stuff happens! Be intentional with your remaining years, create and start living a wonderful life now!

When you think about it, Victory Lap is like a second childhood, where you use your additional years of salary or self-employment income to create new adventures and experiences. Remember back to how we lived when we were young adults. We didn't have a lot of money, but we always seemed to have just enough. We had the ability to eat what we wanted, live where we wanted, travel where we wanted, and we were free from anxiety and fear because everything seemed possible in our minds. We tended to live in the moment and didn't spend a lot of time and energy worrying about what happened yesterday or what tomorrow might bring. In Victory Lap we can start living like kids again, full of life and excitement.

THE BENEFITS OF A VICTORY LAP

There are countless benefits for those who embark on a Victory Lap. Here are nine of the best as far as we're concerned:

1. Victory Lap gives you the opportunity to start over and design a new life for yourself, but without being limited by your job or responsibilities to others. This

time you're doing it for *you* not *them*, and you alone will decide your fate. It's no longer doing what you *have* to do; from now on it's all about what you *want* to do.

2. A Victory Lap Retirement lifestyle reduces fear and anxiety. You will not need to save as much for retirement during your full-time working years, as you are creating a life from which you do not intend to retire anytime soon; you will benefit from continued earnings over a longer period of time. You give yourself the satisfaction of remaining employed to some degree and earning a paycheque, or of becoming self-employed and earning multiple paycheques from a variety of interesting clients.

   One of the biggest risks in traditional retirement is inflation and the loss of purchasing power. At 4 per cent inflation, your buying power halves every eighteen years. Retire at sixty-two, and by age eighty your pension will buy half of what it did at that early retirement age. Most seniors today are putting their savings into low-risk investments like GICs or CDs, which means that, with historically low interest rates, they are safely going broke! Continuing to work, at least a little, will enable you to keep topping up your assets, protecting your nest egg from being slowly eroded by inflation.

3. Moving on from being a good corporate soldier to leading a purposeful life, in which you're doing something you enjoy and that matters to you, may not pay as much in terms of money, but it pays a whole lot more in terms of spiritual meaning, personal health, and length and quality of life. In other words, some amount

of meaningful work in your Victory Lap will keep you
out of the graveyard longer.

4. You can opt to work part-time and free yourself up
    for eldercare, childcare, working out, charitable or
    philanthropic causes, travel, or any number of creative
    pursuits. You'll enjoy far more flexibility even though
    you're still working, and your schedule will be entirely
    under your control—not the Corp's.

5. Victory Lap Retirement gives you the opportunity to do
    the things you had to put off while you raised a family
    and worked toward Findependence. It gives you the
    chance to pursue long-repressed dreams while you're
    still young enough to enjoy them and to create a long,
    successful, and sustainable lifestyle.

6. In Victory Lap Retirement, the goal is to abandon an
    expensive modern way of life and return to a simpler,
    frugal lifestyle. Your Victory Lap allows you to become
    free-spirited, like a kid, again—a time when it seemed
    everything was possible.

7. In Victory Lap, you look for work that combines
    personal meaning and social purpose. The alignment
    of "who you are" with "what you do" is a powerful
    combination that will help maximize both passion and
    happiness. Helping others is the easiest way to get a
    happiness boost. Some may choose to work for pay,
    while others may choose to volunteer. In the end it's
    all about engaging in some form of work that creates
    purpose, gets the creative juices flowing, and gives you

a reason to get out of bed each morning. Victory Lap Retirement will make you happy because you are doing work that you *want* to do. The work you choose will energize rather than deplete you because it's work that doesn't *feel* like work.

8. Victory Lap Retirement is the third act in a four-part play. It's your last shot at creating a happy life, an opportunity to pursue lost dreams and missed opportunities. It gives you the chance to have many extra decades to do good work, enjoy yourself, spend more time with your spouse or partner, and relate in a more meaningful way to your family. It's an incredible chance to have fun, pursue old or new hobbies, make new friends, and possibly start checking off the boxes of your own unique "bucket list."

9. Victory Lap is not about who or what you used to be; it's all about who and what you will become. You should look at it as a rebirth, a "do over," a last shot at doing it right. Don't waste a great opportunity to "finally do it your way."

CREATE A LIFESTYLE PLAN WITH YOUR FINANCIAL ADVISER

It's a surprising fact, but most people do not have a financial plan. Many just rely on the assumption that the more they save for retirement, the better off they will be; while this may seem reasonable, it is not true in all cases. What most people fail to understand is that just achieving a certain level of savings does not guarantee a happy retirement. You cannot assume that because

Joe was happy to hear his financial advisor had
passed the new mandatory B.S. detector test.

you have a good financial plan things will just fall into place when
you retire. Trust us on this, *they won't!*

The truth is that financial planning fails without life planning, and most people do not have a firm handle on what they
are actually saving *for.* If you don't know what you want to do,
how can you and/or your adviser possibly figure out how much
your Victory Lap lifestyle will cost, whether or not you are on
track to save enough to pay for it, or when you can hit your own
Findependence Day?

A good financial adviser will sit down with you and discuss
what you want out of life, then figure out how to build the financial
resources to pay for those things that are important to you. Both
of you need to ensure that the life plan is aligned with the financial plan. The key point is that it's *your* own vision based on your
own plans and dreams; *you* need to be the one designing it, it's not
something you can just delegate to your adviser. You need to hold
yourself accountable for planning a successful Victory Lap.

The biggest challenge people who are leaving the full-time workforce face is figuring out how they are going to spend their next thirty or more years. Leaving your primary career creates a big void in your life: you now must find ways to fill up the fifty extra hours that have been freed up for you every week. You need to create a plan that is designed to keep you challenged, one that will give meaning to your life and provide satisfaction and a sense of accomplishment while also keeping you fit and healthy. If you fail to come up with a plan to fill all of the leisure time available to you each week, you could suffer from self-doubt, regret, lack of purpose, and boredom. And that doesn't sound like a Victory Lap to us.

There are so many interesting lifestyle options available to boomers these days. For example, in their book *Planet Boomer: Retire Now for Less in Southeast Asia*, Jim Herrier and Ellen Ma list fifteen destinations in five Southeast Asian countries that are at least 50 per cent more affordable than the United States or Canada. They also benefit from quality health care and healthy expat communities. Your savings will go a lot further in these places, so you will not need as much annual income if you decide to take a Victory Lap along this path.

You want to look for a financial adviser who offers a holistic approach and can help with the possible non-financial retirement challenges you may face: loss of identity, social/relationship issues, anxiety/depression, or other health issues. It's true what they say, that the two riskiest years in a person's life are the year they were born and the year they retire. And so it can be of great benefit to have someone to talk to, someone who understands what you are going through. Lack of preparedness is often the biggest cause of retirement problems, and good advisers will ensure that their clients are psychologically prepared for retirement. Most retirements fail for non-financial reasons, not financial ones. So be sure that when you're designing a fabulous Victory Lap for yourself, the very first step is figuring out exactly what it is you want out of life once you leave full-time work behind.

TURN YOUR "PAYCHEQUE" INTO A "PLAYCHEQUE"

The beauty of gaining Findependence is that you no longer have to chase after money anymore. Remember, once you're findependent, you are working because you *want* to, not because you *have* to.

Life becomes much easier when you know there is a safety net under you. If you're findependent, all your basic, necessary costs of living are already covered by the passive income from your pensions, government benefits, earnings from your investments, and so on. Think of that passive income as your paycheque, even though you don't get one from a Corp anymore. And look at money earned from the work you might do in your Victory Lap as your fun money that can be used to invest in experiences for you and your family, not money to be used to purchase more "stuff" or to finance your basic needs in retirement. Think of it this way:

ACTIVE (VICTORY LAP) INCOME = FUN MONEY

With all your non-discretionary living expenses covered by your passive income (as outlined in chapter 3), all additional work income can be freely invested into whatever you choose. That is, the money you earn by working even just part-time in your Victory Lap becomes your "playcheque." The beauty here is its simplicity. It's like when you were a kid and could spend only the coins in your pocket, period.

The best route is to open a new fun account and deposit any playcheques derived from your post-Corp work. Just remember that you can't spend more than you earn, so overdrafts on your fun account are definitely not allowed! A fundamental rule in Victory Lap is that we do not want to incur debt or compromise our hard-won Findependence.

FINDING YOUR *IKIGAI*

The challenge is that after having most of your life structured for you while you were working, following orders and doing what you were told, you now need to figure out what you want and how to create a lifestyle that will satisfy you for the rest of your life. That sort of freedom can be daunting for some people. On the positive side, by the time you reach Victory Lap, you will have the benefit of about fifty to sixty years of knowledge, skills, wisdom, insights, and experiences. At this point in your life, you know what you can do and can't do. You know what makes you happy and what doesn't. You know what matters to you and what doesn't. Use this knowledge to create your own version of a successful Victory Lap lifestyle.

Step one is to find work that you love, work that supports how you would really like to live. It should be based on something you enjoy doing, something you are good at, and something for which there is a need. And, ideally, something for which you can be paid! Once you find it, just do it. What are you waiting for? Remember you only get one shot at this.

It's important to understand we're all unique in what we need to be happy; everyone will have their own vision of *ikigai*. Please understand that one person's version is not better than another's. Some might choose to create a Victory Lap that satisfies their basic needs for social interaction and also gives them some extra income. Others, the so-called workaholics, may want their work to play a much larger part in their lives. This may seem to run counter to our goal for a stress-reduced lifestyle, but when you think about it, is it really stressful work if you are doing interesting work that you really enjoy doing? What's wrong with a strong work ethic? What's wrong with completely immersing yourself in a job you love doing?

A LESSON FROM MIKE'S FATHER

I remember when my father decided to retire. He was in charge of a large accounting department that went through a difficult enterprise-wide computer systems conversion late in his career. The constant high stress over a couple of years finally convinced him he had to leave to protect his health. However, being my father, he felt he had an obligation to the company to stay on until the project was completed, even though he suffered from high blood pressure. Staying there too long would have killed him, but as we later learned, leaving to do nothing wouldn't do him any good either. Death by stress or death by boredom—either way you cut it you end up dead!

Finally, he was able to retire when he turned sixty, but almost immediately he began to suffer from sudden retirement syndrome. The shock of leaving a long-term, successful career to do nothing created significant stress for him. He was unprepared for a full-stop retirement, and the drifting and boredom were causing him to lose it. Luckily my mother, who is a very smart woman, threw a copy of the want ads at him with a few opportunities circled. She said, "Here, stop whining and go find something to do." (My mother's Irish, can you tell?) It didn't take long before my father had a new part-time job delivering pet food to people at their homes.

When I first heard what he was doing, I had to laugh. Here was a former corporate executive who at one time had managed a group of about sixty people and now he was having the time of his life delivering pet food. But he didn't stop there. He was concerned about his health, so he decided to start cutting lawns as a side gig to get him into shape and also generate a little bit more fun money. My father had always been frugal and would never pay money to go to a gym, so instead he created his own workout program by cutting lawns, and, boy, was he ever happy with his new lifestyle. Minimal stress, no more deadlines, and he didn't have to manage people anymore.

You see, it doesn't have to be much, it doesn't have to be complicated. It's all up to you and what *you* need to do in order to be happy. Some people view this time of their life as the last chance to chase their dreams; some just want a part-time job to help satisfy their social needs and generate a little extra income. Everyone has different needs and each one of us just has to find the right balance for ourselves, some combination of work and play that will make us happy. And many people have discovered that it doesn't take much at all.

So what can you take away from the story about Mike's father so that you can optimize your own version of Victory Lap?

1. It's important to change the way you view the connection between money and self-worth. Some people think, "I can't do that job, it's below me and will not pay me what I'm worth." In Victory Lap you no longer use money as a measurement, as a way of comparing yourself with others; you simply use it to help finance the things you want to do with your increased leisure time, like going on fun adventures

with your family. Remember, it's your *play*cheque, not your paycheque now.

2. Knowing that you are counted on, that you are valued, gives you a good reason to get up in the morning and will add years to your life. Studies have clearly shown that the sudden loss of a person's traditional role can have a measurable effect on mortality. You die quickly if you feel like you are invisible and are no longer needed. Work—any kind of work—gives you a feeling of responsibility, of making a contribution, of mattering.

3. To ensure a high quality Victory Lap, it's important to socialize and have the benefit of a social network. Work gives you the chance to surround yourself with fun, interesting people.

A LESSON FROM JONATHAN'S FATHER

My Dad experienced a much different traditional retirement than Mike's. After fighting World War II in England as a naval officer, he emigrated with his bride to Canada, where my brother and I were born. After a series of manual labour jobs, he got his B.A. and ended up as a high school English and French teacher. He retired from the Ontario teaching system and started to collect the famously lucrative teacher pension before going on to spend a few extra years building his nest egg by teaching in Nova Scotia and in effect double-dipping (drawing an Ontario teacher's pension and a Nova Scotia teacher's salary at the same time). When he finally did completely retire in his mid-sixties, he never looked back. He was utterly content collecting the pension and spending his time reading, walking, and socializing. That was his idea of a Victory Lap. End of lesson!

THE IT'S-TOO-LATE TRAP

An all-too-common phenomenon is what we call the "it's too late" trap. It doesn't seem to matter what age you are and what life dream you've been postponing, an oft-used rationalization tends to be something like, "Well, if I had only started activity X back when I was twenty, things would be different. But now that I'm [plug in your current age here], it's just too late to make a change."

Now it's true that certain professions are best entered while you have a young and healthy body. We don't know too many athletes who decide to become NHL hockey players after the age of thirty-five or forty, for example. But if you're a modern office-dwelling "knowledge worker" or "symbol manipulator," odds are you're mostly using your mind, not your body. If anything, the mind just gets stronger with use over the years and your cranium gets filled with all sorts of knowledge a younger person may not possess.

The subtitle to Joyce Meyer's book *You Can Begin Again* is also the book's key message: *No Matter What, It's Never Too Late.* Meyer discovered that this theme runs throughout the Bible, although it certainly also applies to daily life. It turns out that doors may close for a reason, but as the old saying goes, when one does close, you can be sure another is sure to open soon after. You may think you've come up with a plan, call it Plan A, but Meyer points out that unbeknownst to you, the Almighty may already have put into motion Plan B. And the B stands for "Better!" In this way, failure (or perceived failure, like being fired, a business failing, or a divorce) can clear the way and set you up for future success.

Earlier in the book we talked about breakthroughs in human longevity and, therefore, rising life expectancies. We've described the likelihood of many of us enjoying a longer lifespan and, therefore, a longer workspan. We've described a whole new stage of life that we call the Victory Lap—which may occur after you leave the corporate stage and have established a modicum of Findependence, but which may be decades before what we used to call traditional "full-stop" retirement.

The Victory Lap concept is another way to view encore careers. The point is that it's never too late to launch an encore act and rev your engines for a satisfying Victory Lap. Try to rid yourself of the notion that fifty years old (or sixty, seventy, or any other age) is "too old" or "too late" to start something new. Nonsense! Odds are that if you take care of yourself, eat properly, exercise regularly, avoid smoking and other life-shortening habits, you'll have an excellent chance of reaching age 100. If so, then fifty is just the half-way mark! You'd have fifty more years to retrain and launch your encore career, and even to master that new calling and become one of the world's leading practitioners of it.

The encore-career literature is full of examples of supposedly "old" people who launched the career that gained them world fame only after they had reached the age of traditional retirement. Anna Mary Robertson "Grandma" Moses, who began painting in earnest at seventy-eight; or fast food kings Ray Kroc and Colonel Harland Sanders, both of whom launched their firms (McDonald's and Kentucky Fried Chicken, respectively) after their fiftieth birthdays. There are many more similar examples. So if you catch yourself saying, "It's too late to start anything new," do what mothers used to do to their children who let loose swear words. Wash your mouth out with soap!

Come to view the phrase "it's too late" as nothing more than what it actually is: an excuse for staying in your rut and refusing to face your fears and conquer them. It's just another dream-killer. So whatever it is you dream of doing—be it learning a musical instrument; writing a novel or a screenplay; or becoming a rock star or a painter or an actor or an ordained minister or an in-demand platform speaker or any of a thousand other possible encore careers—just grit your teeth and start doing it.

Have, Do, Be

Remember this simple formula: Have, do, be. The first step is obtaining the tool or instrument required to practice your new craft. It may be a piano, a guitar, a palette and paints, or a computer equipped with a word processor. Having acquired the tool, you need to use it: do the painting, do the writing, play the musical instrument. And after a period of doing it, you will one day realize that you have become this new person: you *are* a painter, writer, or musician, and an entire new career is launched—perhaps one that will not only be satisfying, but one that may also carry the bonus of paying you for practicing it. Recall the song from the cult film, *The Rocky Horror Picture Show*, and the classic lyric, "Don't dream it. Be it." Too late to dream it? Balderdash! Have, do, be.

6

Create a Life from Which You Don't Have to Retire

The biggest adventure you can ever take is to live the life of your dreams.
  —*Oprah Winfrey*

No one could accuse Oprah Winfrey of failing to think big and live the life of her dreams. Despite the odds against her when she started out, Oprah became a one-woman media empire. She has passed age sixty and, even though her net worth is in the billions, she shows little sign of wishing to retire because she loves what she does. Why would any of us want to retire if we found something that we can be passionate about, even if we have somewhat less wealth than the famous Ms. Winfrey? The challenge is to find out what your innermost dreams are, then create a life from which you may never want to retire, as long as you are physically and mentally able to keep up the pace (even if a slightly more leisurely pace than your primary career).

The most common term used to describe late-life career changes is an encore career, often termed an encore act or second act. There are many great resources for boomers interested in

Work while you play, play while you work.

finding or creating an encore career. You could start by typing either of those terms on Amazon.com. One book you'll find, and which we highly recommend, is Marc Freedman's *Encore: Finding Work that Matters in the Second Half of Life.* Also check out the companion website that Freedman founded at Encore.org and, for a Canadian perspective, take a look www.challengefactory.ca.

Once you have done the homework and identified what route you want to take in your Victory Lap, you'll need to create a plan based on prudent, well-researched moves prior to jumping into it.

KEY CONSIDERATIONS

Following are some important things to consider when planning your Victory Lap.

1. The best time to plan for Victory Lap Retirement is a few years prior to achieving Findependence. Prior to jumping off (as discussed in chapter 3) we strongly recommend starting your Victory Lap only after you have reached your Findependence Day.

2. Find a job or create one that matches up with the skills and talents that are your strengths. Play to your strengths whenever possible.

3. Identify any additional education, skills, and training required prior to starting your Victory Lap, then work on adding them to your Victory Lap Retirement arsenal.

4. Find work you are passionate about, something you are proud of and which is important to you. It should be work you find challenging and interesting, that awakens your creativity and may even provide an acceptable level of income. Avoid doing something you do not enjoy. Seek work that lets you see the personal contribution you are making and the results that flow from that contribution.

5. Identify mentors, and reach out to your network of social and professional contacts for help and guidance. Surround yourself with positive, supportive people. Create a support team that will cheer you on and help you get there. Talk to those who have already gone there and done it. Often other people can see a solution that you can't because they are not as emotionally invested in the situation; you're just too close to your own situation to judge. This is where a good money coach, financial adviser, or even a life coach or soul coach may be of great benefit. Don't be too proud to ask for help if you need it.

6. Find a role model and copy what he or she did. If that person did it, why can't you?

7. You need to do your homework and come up with an idea, then research options about how to make it happen before you pull the trigger. Have someone review your plan and test it for soundness. Take a calculated risk rather than throwing caution to the wind. At this time in your life, you don't have as long to recover from a financial setback, so do your best to minimize the risk and maximize your chances of success going into your Victory Lap.

8. If possible, take some time off before starting your Victory Lap. You need to be mentally ready to make the change. Take a breather of perhaps three months so you can regroup, recharge, and collect yourself. This is like taking a racehorse and putting it on the farm for a "freshening period" after a long, hard campaign. Tired horses don't run well, and neither will you. In these days of corporate restructuring, the severance package that often accompanies layoffs can give both precious time and money to contemplate your next move. By all means, at least take a week or two vacation first, then enter research-and-networking mode.

9. To start your Victory Lap, you need to get physically fit and create an energetic appearance and mindset. When you are fit you feel good, and people pick up on the positive vibes you are sending out. We all like people with a positive attitude, and we're drawn to them.

10. Last but certainly not least, make sure your spouse or partner is onside!

YOUR VICTORY LAP IS LIMITED
ONLY BY YOUR IMAGINATION

There isn't enough space here to do justice to the various options available in a typical Victory Lap trajectory, and new ones are being created all the time. Scenarios range from the story of Professor Fred Kummerow and the people employed at Vita Needle (see chapter 1) to the lifestyle created by Mike's father, who got joy and satisfaction out of delivering pet food and other odd jobs. The point we're trying to make is that the lifestyle you create is unique to you: all that matters is that it's meaningful and that it works for you and only you.

Some of the more interesting Victory Lap stories, a sampling of which follows here, involve a degree of seasonality and could really be thought of as forms of mini-retirement.

- After leaving his corporate job, Don—a self-professed golf nut—found employment at a high-end golf club during the summer. In addition to hanging out with golfers and talking about golf all day, one of the perks for Don is that he can golf for free. He and his wife spend their winters in Mexico, where he spends most of his time playing, you guessed it, golf.

- Frank, on the other hand, just loves to fish. Soon after retirement he bought a small fishing lodge up north. In a good year he barely breaks even, but he just loves fishing and hanging out with other fishermen. He spends his winters in Belize, where his wife relaxes while he fly fishes for bonefish.

- Harry and his wife owned their own clothing business but sold it when Harry turned sixty-seven. His wife was the first to go back to work, working part-time at a store that specialized in wedding dresses. Harry followed soon after once he completed the sale of their large home and the process of downsizing to a condo. He just celebrated his twentieth year working in a store specializing in suits for kids, where he just loves interacting with the parents.

• John is an artist who's pretty handy with tools. He's built a business building and selling sheds and Muskoka chairs while at his cottage in the summer.

• Ron, who was always good with a guitar, went on vacation one year to St. Martin and decided to stay. He started playing at a restaurant on the boardwalk to help attract new customers from all the passengers coming off the many cruise ships that visit each winter. Ron, one might say, has the life of Riley!

• Frank and Jenny, both former computer analysts, now provide assistance to people who want to sell items online. They guide their clients every step of the way through the process.

• Lara is one of those people who understands everything computer-related. She assisted one of this book's co-authors in setting up a website and creating a blog. She is the go-to person when you want to do anything with a computer.

• Jim and Ellen left successful careers in marketing and advertising and are now serving as explorers, scouting areas in Southeast Asia where boomers can enjoy an affordable retirement. They have their own blog, www.planet-boomer.com, and have recently written a book about their adventures called *Planet Boomer: Retire Now for Less in Southeast Asia.*

MONETIZING A HOBBY

If you're still in your primary career it's a good idea to consider starting a side business or perhaps monetizing a hobby. (Some call this turning an avocation into a vocation!) You know that eventually you will end up here anyway, so why not give yourself a head start? Also, if by chance something happens to your primary career, you could lean on the cash flow from your side business until you find another gig.

Look at Joe, for example. He used his woodworking hobby as a way to decompress from his gruelling office job. Eventually he built his own cottage. When he was asked to leave his corporate career, he started to generate some cash flow doing the odd renovation for some neighbours. Today, he happily spends his summers at the cottage doing renovations for other cottagers. By the time winter comes, he's in Costa Rica with his wife. Let's just say Joe can't keep himself from smiling!

Some may argue that they don't have time to do so much, but think about just how much time we all waste every day. The average American watches more than 1,600 hours of television each year, which is the equivalent of 200 eight-hour work days. If you applied the same amount of time to starting a part-time business, you would be far ahead of the average American. Imagine, through the power of compounding, what you could accomplish over a ten-year period. Stop thinking and just start—now.

START YOUR OWN BUSINESS

All our dreams can come true if we have the courage to pursue them.
    —*Walt Disney*

A dream is your creative vision for your life in the future. You must break out of your current comfort zone and become comfortable with the unfamiliar and the unknown.
    —*Denis Waitley*

If you accept the thesis that, in general, people will continue to live longer than was once anticipated, it hardly seems unreasonable for financially independent baby boomers who have left giant corporations to embrace a brand new work life. As we make clear in this book at several junctures, if you believe your health is robust enough to put you in the extended life expectancy camp, it's definitely not too late to try something new if you've only just reached your fifties or sixties. Try thinking of yourself as being merely at the halfway mark of life, with decades of healthy living—and working—ahead of you.

Our term for late-bloomer baby boomer entrepreneurs is "Boomerpreneur." Boomerpreneurs are free to follow their dreams. They are like starving artists who care more about their art than the pursuit of material wealth, except they aren't starving, because they have achieved Findependence. Knowing that your basic needs are met—whether it be the funds for food, utilities, property taxes, and the like—frees you up to take on longer-term projects: projects like writing a book or creating a website like the Financial Independence Hub (to cite just two examples near and dear to our hearts!).

Boomerpreneurs are builders who try to create something, perhaps something they dreamed about for most of their lives but never had the chance to attempt. Dreams are powerful: they energize your mind, ignite your passion, and drive you to do everything you can in order to achieve them. Chasing after a dream and finally catching it is one of the happiest and most fulfilling things you could ever do.

In Victory Lap, Boomerpreneurs know exactly where they want to go, what is important to them, what they want, and what will make them happy. They gain strength from knowing that after so many years they are finally in control of their own destiny. Now *they're* the ones who make the big decisions.

Benefits of Being a Boomerpreneur

Below are some of the top advantages that come with being self-employed.

1. Satisfaction derived from being in control of your work and being your own boss. It's your business, done your way.

2. Ability to create your own work–life balance. A key benefit is the flexibility this lifestyle allows. You're able to set your own hours, so you can work hard when you want to, take time off when you feel like it, and sometimes even work in your pajamas if you want to.

3. You constantly challenge yourself. You compete, learn new things and, as a result, grow.

4. You increase the size of your social circle by connecting with your clients and suppliers.

5. You can choose who you want to work with and surround yourself with positive people who care about you.

6. Building your own business, helping others, and being successful gives a big boost to you in terms of personal satisfaction. When you help others you really are helping yourself.

How about an Internet-based Business?

Back in the 1960s or 70s when the boomers were starting their careers, a huge amount of capital was required to start a business, often hundreds of thousands of dollars to cover equipment, staff salaries, renting workspace, inventory, and other major costs.

Today, anyone with a computer and access to the World Wide Web can start their own Internet-based business, and the cost is almost negligible—potentially as little as $20 or $30 a month to get started.

It doesn't matter how old you are or how healthy you are, the Internet has no biases. You can run an online business out of your home, at Starbucks, or anywhere in the world that has an Internet connection. You can work on projects that you are passionate about, start a blog, self-publish a book, become a consultant, or sell things. You can make money on your own schedule and control your own income by how hard and how well you do your job. How cool is that?

This is one reason we envy the millennials or children of the boomers. They can bypass the whole corporate experience if they identify an online niche early on and pursue it. (The name Mark Zuckerberg comes to mind here.) But being self-employed comes with its own hurdles. Unlike working in a salaried position, Boomerpreneurs need to create something and ship the product or do the work involved before they make any money. It takes time to start up a new business and start seeing a return on your efforts—far more time than if you worked strictly for a salary.

If you decide to become a Boomerpreneur, it's important to understand that out of the gate your Victory Lap could result in a sizeable pay cut until your business gains traction. This is one big reason we advocate launching your Victory Lap only after you have achieved Findependence. Before you start leading the Victory Lap lifestyle, it would be wise to focus on paying off your big expenses. Wait until the kids are out of college, the mortgage is paid off, and you are out of debt. Consider the possibility of downsizing. Always have a back-up plan in case things don't work out. Do you have the cushion of a partner's income to act as a safety net so you can sleep at night?

TRANSITIONS CAN TAKE LONGER THAN YOU THINK

There's a good chance your original plan or business model will not be the one you finally end up with; plans evolve, so be open to tweaking things. Always listen to and go with your inner voice. If it's telling you that you need to change things, then go ahead and make the required changes. At some point your inner voice will whisper that you are attracted to something. You feel excitement, a sense of alignment, happiness, clarity, a knowing that this is the thing, the right thing for you to do. Don't be afraid. Just do it!

This change of direction is exactly what happened to Mike after he joined his wife's wealth management business. At first he had planned on becoming an investment adviser focusing on succession planning for family-owned businesses. But as he talked to more and more people, he felt the need to help others with their fear of retirement and assist them with their transition into their own version of a Victory Lap. Having never written before, he never would have considered writing blogs, nor for that matter helping to write the book you are currently holding. Funny how plans change!

TAKE YOUR VICTORY LAP OUT FOR A TEST DRIVE

We test drive many things in our lives, from cars to relationships, before making long-term commitments. So it makes sense to test drive your version of Victory Lap prior to leaving your primary career, to ensure that it works *for* you rather than *against* you. Victory Lap is a huge unknown, but you can increase the odds of creating an enjoyable one if you spend the time to test it out before actually taking the plunge. We recommend that you start your test period three to five years before you actually leave the Corp behind, with emphasis on the following areas during the test period:

1. Confirm that you can afford your new lifestyle. Test drive living on your Victory Lap budget. Does it meet your expectations?

2. Take a vacation in the location where you plan to reside eventually. If you're going to spend winters in Mexico, test out your planned community when you're on vacation from the Corp.

3. Try to test your Victory Lap gig. Talk to people already doing it. Try to shadow someone who is doing what you want to be doing in your Victory Lap. Or do your future encore job part-time while you are still in your primary career.

4. Test your future daily routines. Were you bored?

After a test drive, you will be able to hit the ground running when you start your Victory Lap. You may also be pleasantly surprised to learn that a successful Victory Lap isn't linked to having tons of money, but rather it is linked to living a more interesting, simpler, less expensive and less stressful lifestyle—on your own terms.

SHOULD YOU ANNOUNCE YOUR PLANS FOR A VICTORY LAP?

Of course you're incredibly excited when you hit upon that purpose to which you want to dedicate the next phase of your life, when you're juiced by the prospect of a new part-time career or when you can't wait to be in control of your own schedule and your own destiny in your Victory Lap. Naturally you want to share your exciting plans with everyone around you, including your colleagues in the Corp you're leaving, and maybe even your boss. But be careful, bosses can start to act a little strangely after you tell them you plan to leave the company at some point in the future.

It's an unfair assumption, but upon hearing of your future intentions your boss may believe you are no longer fully committed to your job and that your performance will start to slide as you focus on getting ready for your new career. This can cause some friction, so it's best to make sure you have the bulk of your Victory Lap preparation completed prior to dropping the bomb, just in case.

In Mike's case, within three months of having declared he was planning to leave, he was pleasantly surprised to receive a buyout from the company. Was it a coincidence? Who knows, but it's better to receive a payout than a gold watch any day. The bonus is that Mike's lump-sum payment generated some liquidity until his new business started to generate a profit.

MOVING FROM BUILDING WEALTH
TO DRAWING AN INCOME

In Victory Lap (or even in traditional retirement), the focus shifts from wealth accumulation to wealth de-accumulation or, as it's often called, decumulation. (There is even a company with a website devoted to this topic: Decumulation Institute at www.decumulation.ca.)

When you look back at the financial life cycle through which most of us progress (see chapter 4), there is a certain yin and yang to some of the phases. The yin of accumulation in the early years is counterbalanced by the yang of decumulation in the later years. Similarly, while we say for those in the family formation stage that the foundation of financial independence is a paid-for home, at some point in Victory Lap you may want to downsize and extract some capital from your principal residence.

The skillset required for decumulation is quite different than wealth accumulation, and this goes not just for you but also your financial adviser. For your part, your mindset needs to switch suddenly from saving as much as you can to starting to spend all of that hard-earned money you've been so careful to invest for so many years. It may sound like fun, easy even, but making that mental shift can be very tough for a lot of people.

As for your adviser, you may find that the person who helped get you to Findependence may not be as well equipped for the decumulation phase. It's important that your financial adviser is equipped with specialized knowledge and different skills to guide you through the financial issues you'll face in this phase of your life. For example, the adviser must be much more concerned with helping you to preserve your capital and minimize the impact of taxation. If you check out the blogs of EmeritusFinancial.com's Doug Dahmer that are on the Hub or you read Daryl Diamond's book *Your Retirement Income Blueprint: A Six-Step Plan to Design and Build a Secure Retirement,* you'll see that both financial experts report that one of the biggest expenses in retirement is taxation. It takes an adviser with special skills to optimize after-tax cash flow from multiple sources of income. When to commence the flow of benefits from corporate pensions, Social Security in the United States, or CPP/OAS in Canada; when to convert tax-sheltered plans like IRAs or RRSPs to income-generation; and how to optimize tax-free vehicles like Roth plans or TFSAs are all part of this increasingly complex subject.

That's not the focus of this book, but the sources above are excellent places to start, as is the aforementioned book by Frederick Vettese, *The Essential Retirement Guide,* and the international edition of Moshe Milevsky's and Alexandra Macqueen's *Pensionize Your Nest Egg: How to Use Product Allocation to Create a Guaranteed Income for Life.* These last two books are written for both Americans and Canadians, as is the book that you are now reading.

When people enter Victory Lap they normally go from having one source of active income (their job) to having multiple sources of cash flow, both passive (pensions, government benefits, investment income) and active (revenue from their encore career or part-time job). Some may even have to draw down some of their invested capital in order to generate the cash flow they require over this period. Some of the considerations that need to be reviewed are:

- Which income streams should be accessed and in what order?

- Which assets should be used first and which ones deferred for later use?

- How can we minimize taxes paid and preserve government entitlements?

At this point in your life, it's not just about investing in stocks and bonds and holding for the long run. You now have to worry about drawing income in a tax-efficient manner and from a variety of income sources. Remember, the single biggest expense in retirement is likely to be taxes, and it's not just how much you take out that affects the size of the bill, it's also the order in which you tap your different income sources, and the mix at any given time! (Try playing the "Retirement Tax Game," which you can find in one of Dahmer's blogs on the Hub, to see what the tax impact is of various retirement income scenarios.)

SOME RULES TO LIVE BY IN VICTORY LAP

To ensure you have a successful Victory Lap, you need to be aware of and address the following:

1. Make sure you have created a sufficient combination of passive and active income to fund the lifestyle that you want in Victory Lap. Take the guesswork out of the equation.

2. Do everything you can to simplify, declutter, and consolidate, so that you can be free to spend more time on the things that are really important to you.

3. Victory Laps don't just happen; you need to *make* yours happen. Have specific plans and goals in place that are in harmony with what you want out of this phase of your life. Have a good reason to get out of bed in the morning. If you don't have specific plans and goals, chances are you will fall into a boring routine, consisting of sleeping in and watching excessive amounts of TV. Don't settle for *Friends* reruns when retirement can be so much more.

4. There will be some bumps in the road at the beginning of your Victory Lap; there always are when you start something new. Understand that it takes time to be really good at something and with practice things will work out.

5. Inherent in the image of a Victory Lap is a journey, so don't settle for standing still. Keep investing in yourself and never quit learning. Learning is a key element to an interesting, rewarding Victory Lap: it helps you discover new things; it facilitates you meeting new people with whom you can interact; it provides personal satisfaction and a sense of accomplishment. Be a lifelong learner and challenge yourself every day.

6. Be intentional with your Victory Lap and spend your time wisely. Stay connected with others and remember that curiosity is what keeps you growing. Successful Victory Lappers focus purposefully on growing and maintaining their physical, mental, and spiritual well-being. Failed retirees just take what comes.

7. Keeping happy and fulfilled over the next thirty years doesn't happen from one single set of actions; you must keep working at it. Hang out with interesting people who are full of life. Avoid people who complain and feel sorry for themselves.

8. You don't need to travel the world in order to experience a fulfilling retirement. You can enjoy having a great retirement right in your own backyard. Design the Victory Lap that's right for *you*.

9. Make a commitment to a healthy lifestyle so you can maximize the length and quality of your Victory Lap. Remember that quality beats quantity every time.

10. Slow things down, stop chasing money so intently, get back to the basics, take time to enjoy the smell of your morning coffee, and realize once again what a wonderful world this really is.

11. In Victory Lap you will be faced with many challenges, but always remember that is what makes life interesting and really worth living. If everything were to come easily, why bother doing it? Just remember, in your Victory Lap you are finally writing your own story, blazing your own trail into the future, and the best is yet to come!

Victory Lap lets you re-imagine your life, and allows for renewal and adventure. Who cares what others think? This time it is *your* choice, *your* rules, *your* way. It won't always be easy—the best things in life never are—but with effort comes a sense of accomplishment, which makes the victory in the end so much sweeter. After all, life without challenge and purpose is really not much of a life at all.

7

Goal Setting and the Pursuit of Happiness

Are You Aligned?

The best way to predict the future is to create it.
—Abraham Lincoln

If you do what you've always done, you'll get what you've always gotten.
—Anthony Robbins

The quote above by Abraham Lincoln is something of which we should all remind ourselves every day. We all have the power within us to control our destiny, but we often forget this as we become overwhelmed by life's complexities. We're so busy with day-to-day living that we don't have time to stop and think about what we really want out of our life and how we can make our dreams a reality. We assume that if we go to work, follow orders, and work hard, everything will work out in the end, but this is one of the biggest mistakes we can make.

Many people allow their lives simply to happen to them, focusing only on getting through the next day, week, or month. Years fly by and valuable time is wasted, until the day they eventually wake up and wish they had taken charge of their life and set goals earlier. To avoid this from happening to you, you need to know what you want out of life, then figure out a way to get there. That goes as much for planning your retirement as it does for any other time in your life, although it's arguably even more important when planning your Victory Lap, to ensure you avoid drifting aimlessly through your later years. When you have a full-time job, goals and structure are imposed on you even if you don't create them for yourself. When that employment suddenly ends, you have to set your own goals and structure your life for yourself.

Setting goals restores a sense of focus in a world that has become complicated by too many options and distractions, and it provides a sense of purpose, particularly for those faced with the blank slate of retirement. Goals clarify our desires and help us focus on those activities that will lead us to where we want to go. Goals and plans take the worry and stress out of living: you'll know exactly where you want to go and how you'll get there because you have a plan aligned with your objectives. Goals commit you to a course of action. Setting goals that engage and motivate you is one of the best ways to boost the level of your personal commitment to life and bring energy to your days.

Happiness comes from knowing where you want to go and why, setting worthy goals, and achieving them as you follow the game plan for your life. Happiness comes from knowing that you gave life your best shot!

FAILING TO PLAN IS PLANNING TO FAIL

Those who set goals and prepare plans to achieve them succeed in life. Setting a goal and not creating and following a plan to achieve it is merely a wish. Hope is not a strategy; a well-thought-out plan is. Following are some recommended steps that will help guide you in planning your Victory Lap goals.

Step 1: Articulate Your Dream for Victory Lap

The first step is to articulate your vision for your own personal Victory Lap, one that will allow you to live the longest, healthiest, most interesting, and most satisfying life that you can. All of your dreams and goals must be aligned with what you want to accomplish in life and with what you wish to become.

Once you have determined what you are passionate about, you need to make your goals come alive in your imagination.

Visualize exactly what you want to do and where you want to go. The more vivid the image, the stronger your desire to get there will be. Our vision delivers to us our *ikigai*, or reason why we get out of bed each morning. Dream large and feel your happiness and energy start to flow.

Step 2: Establish Your Core Goals

Core goals are themes that form the code you choose to live by in order to achieve your vision. Think about the accomplishments you would want talked about in your eulogy: "She loved life," "He cared and always put his family first," "He was a generous man." Visualize your legacy after you're gone and how those who survive you will describe that legacy: how you had helped others, showed compassion, and made contributions to your community.

Core goals are based on what a person wants to accomplish in life, not in terms of making money or acquiring more stuff, but how you can help and touch the souls of others.

Step 3: Establish Your Short-term Goals

Short-term goals serve as stepping stones that help us realize our long-term vision for a healthy Victory Lap lifestyle. From longevity studies we know which areas in our lives we need to address—the things we need to do to keep engaged, healthy, and balanced. We need to take that knowledge and convert it into clear and well-defined sub-goals so that we, too, can live a long life.

These short-term goals will become the "how," the steps you will take to achieve the bigger vision you have of the kind of Victory Lap you want to run. The key in establishing short-term goals is to make sure they are clearly articulated: write them down, set a specific completion date, and hold yourself accountable.

Examples of short-term goals include:
- Achieve Findependence by December 31, 2018
- Meditate for thirty minutes each morning commencing February 1, 2016
- Lose thirty pounds by December 31, 2016
- Restrict television viewing to one hour a day commencing April 1, 2016
- Volunteer to help organize the local hospital charity run on April 1, 2017

Tracking your progress on a spreadsheet and regularly comparing it with your goals will serve to motivate you and ensure that you stay on track. For example, plotting your quarterly spend rate versus your quarterly passive income level will indicate how quickly you are approaching your own Findependence Day. When the lines intersect, that's your time for a big party!

The real value of setting and achieving goals lies not so much in the rewards you receive but *in the person you become* as a result of reaching your goals. Celebrate the fact that the process of reaching your short-term goal has improved the person that you are. You have built self-discipline, discovered new things about yourself, and realized more of your human potential. Not a bad deal! And as you begin achieving the goals you've set for yourself, continue to develop new ones. Remember, your Victory Lap is a purposeful journey—don't stand still.

THE ANNUAL REVIEW

Every year between Christmas and New Year's, Mike and the Contessa sit down and review their personalized "road map," the goals they set for themselves annually. This road map is broken down into a number of categories: health, family, money, experiences, top ten list, good/bad habits, and so on. They review the goals they have accomplished over the past year and establish new goals to ensure continual progress toward their ultimate goal of "an awesome Victory Lap lifestyle." They make a list of the special events that will be coming up—birthdays, anniversaries, special occasions, holidays—and plan ways to make them unique and memorable. Family experiences are where you want to invest your time. The payback in terms of personal satisfaction is huge!

Here's an example of how Mike set short-term goals that aligned with one of his major objectives: to help people through sharing advice and offering encouragement and hope in his writing (both through this book and his blog). As Malcolm Gladwell posits in his book *Outliers: The Story of Success*, it takes approximately 10,000 hours to become a master at anything. Based on this idea, Mike calculated that the realization of his major goal would take him on a journey over a ten-year period. Following are the short-term goals he plans to meet to help him get there:

1. To stay productive over those ten years, he established fitness and nutritional goals to ensure he would remain healthy and maintain high energy during that period.

2. To create awareness of the concept behind Victory Lap, Mike established the goal of writing this book with Jonathan, and together we set a tentative completion date of June 2016.

3. Both of us had independently joined the local chapters of Toastmasters International, which will come in handy when it comes time to market this book and speak at seminars about it. (As one of Jonathan's publishing friends once quipped, "Books don't sell themselves!")

4. Mike also set a goal of writing blogs for the Findependence Hub in order to help create even more awareness for the book.

To live well and succeed in life you need to be intentional, purposeful, and work continually toward a worthy goal that you set for yourself. You can't expect a positive outcome if you don't have a viable plan. Without goals you're at the mercy of whatever happens. The simple truth is that successful people succeed because they know where they want to go and how to get there.

ALIGNING DAILY HABITS WITH LONG-TERM GOALS

We are what we repeatedly do. Excellence then, is not an action, but a habit.
    —*Aristotle*

Motivation is what gets you going. Habit is what keeps you going.
    —*Jim Rohn*

The goals we set for ourselves are important drivers, motivating us to achieve the big things we want out of life. So it's amazing to note that, according to the results of a Duke University study conducted in 2006, more than 40 per cent of our days are actually controlled by habits and routines that we have created for ourselves over the years. Over time, habits become part of our daily rituals and we are no longer conscious of the routine being carried out. Habits and routines cause us to do things the same way every day.

Think about when you take a shower and the routine you have developed over the years. Your routine is carried out without conscious thought; but see what happens when you disrupt the pattern by thinking about something else while you are performing the task. How many times has this happened to you? You can't remember whether you shampooed your hair or not because your normal routine, which is usually on autopilot, was disrupted by some distracting thought that entered your mind. The fact is that most of us are on autopilot for most of the day.

Whereas goal setting is intentional and can lead to feelings of accomplishment, purpose, and fulfillment, habits are unconscious and automatic; they control our daily lives to a great degree, which can lead to boredom, aimlessness, apathy, general unease, and sometimes much more unhealthy consequences.

Of course, there are good habits and there are bad habits. Most of the time it's pretty easy to tell them apart and to know which ones you ought to adopt and which ones you should stay away from. For instance, you know that eating multiple servings of fruits and vegetables every day is a good habit to get into, and that smoking is a habit you should break or avoid. But even good or benign habits can lead you astray if they are not aligned with your long-term goals and if they are not intentional.

The thing is, you're unlikely to achieve a goal unless your habits support it. Therefore, if your existing daily habits are not aligned with your long-term goal, you'll need to change your habits in order to reach your goal. When you set a goal, think about what habits you need to change or what would allow you to put the obtainment of that goal on autopilot. For instance, if you wanted to save a certain amount of money to take a much-needed vacation, you might consider eliminating your "retail therapy" habit of walking the malls on the weekend. Or instead of going out for an expensive lunch every day of the week, perhaps you choose to bring a healthy lunch to work. You will end up saving lots of money and getting healthier at the same time.

Adopting and maintaining good habits is hard enough at the best of times, and harder still when you're surrounded by the noise of advertisers tempting you in their direction. Consumer marketers spend millions upon millions of dollars studying the effect of habits, using what they learn to help them market the tons of (largely unnecessary) products we consume every year. They understand how the average person responds to the marketing of luxury products, and they use this information to try to trap us in a habitual purchasing routine. In other words, they put a spell over you and turn your family into consumer zombies.

Advertisers know that most of us are unwilling to spend much time and effort on something after we've endured another long, hard day at the office. Why do you think they created mail-in rebate programs? They know many of us will not expend the energy to mail in the rebates, even though it means saving money. How dumb (or smart) is that? Advertisers know our own habits better than we do.

That's why it's important to fully understand the power that your habits hold over you and to find ways to change them so you can regain control over your life. Unbeknownst to you, habits will take you in a particular direction—potentially one you do not really wish to go in—so it's important to ensure that your habits are aligned with your dreams. Choose your habits intentionally, or they will choose your destiny for you.

Over time, habits become automatic and take little effort, so you don't need to think much about what you are doing. This is fine if the habit in question is healthy, but if it's a negative habit it

Within a few short months of retiring,
Mike started to look like Howard Hughes...

could destroy you if it continues long enough. According to the 2012 *Medscape Physician Lifestyle Report*, 44 per cent of doctors are overweight, even though they are well aware of the importance of regular exercise and good nutrition. Knowing what to do is meaningless if you are unwilling to spend the effort and put the right habits in place.

Changing a habit is often easier said than done, as it takes a certain amount of self-discipline. In his book *The Power of Habit: Why We Do What We Do in Life and Business*, Charles Duhigg reveals ways to help change these powerful routines. Habits start with a trigger and end with a reward that reinforces the habit. The best way to change a habit is to keep the same trigger and reward but change the pattern in between. According to Duhigg, here are some steps you should take to invoke habit change:

1. **Determine the trigger for your habit.**
   For instance, say you have developed the habit of
   drinking a beer or two while you barbeque your dinner.
   The habit of having a beer is triggered by the lighting of
   the barbecue.

2. **Use the same trigger, but replace the routine with a**
   different behaviour.
   So instead of opening a beer after lighting the barbecue,
   you could talk to your family and see how their day
   went or you could pick some weeds out of the garden or
   water your lawn.

3. **Keep the reward similar to the old one.**
   After having a beer you feel relaxed, so make sure
   after you barbecue that you sit down and decompress
   however you want. Instead of a beer, enjoy a coffee or
   perhaps an iced tea.

The key is to understand your habits and how they control your
life. Awareness will allow you to find ways to create positive
change. Always be aware of what is happening around you, why
it's happening, and how it can impact you. Stay in the moment, be
aware of it, and you will be much better off for it.

A useful exercise is to list all the bad things that could happen
if you don't change the bad habits, then list all the good things
that will occur if you make the required changes. When you start
with the end in mind, it's easier to analyze each choice closely and
make the smart choice so you can achieve your goals.

Once you create a habit, good or bad, over time that habit
starts to control you. It's important to understand that habits are
not temporary; it becomes very difficult to delete a programmed

behaviour. You must strive to adopt only habits that in the long run will be beneficial rather than destructive to you. Your quality of life will be determined in large measure by the nature of your habits. The key is to ensure that your habits move you forward rather than hold you back. For example, you know you need to institute proper lifestyle habits in order to meet the goal of increased longevity. And so you must get in the habit of eating right, exercising, and socializing regularly with family and friends. The bottom line is that you need to be intentional and create everyday habits aligned with your long-term goals.

MIKE'S CHANGING HABITS

I was concerned when I set the long-term goal of having an amazing and fulfilling Victory Lap that there were certain habits in my life that were working against my goal. I am in the process of trying to change these habits for the better, to ensure that my Victory Lap is vibrant, rewarding, sustainable, and fun.

1. **Exercise:** Because I want to enjoy a healthy life for as long as possible, I needed to adopt a more active lifestyle. Recently I started to walk outdoors with the Contessa; the game plan is to transition into a walk/run program with the ultimate goal of completing a half marathon.

   Also, instead of driving everywhere, I plan on biking whenever possible, whether to the gym, library, or shopping mall. By adopting a disciplined exercise program I will lose weight, gain energy, and hopefully get myself off the blood pressure pills I have been taking.

2. **Nutrition:** I've always been a meat-and-potatoes guy and there has never been much room on my plate for vegetables

or other healthy foods. But I have awoken to the evil of my ways and decided to work hard in this area. More fish, salad, and fruit and less booze. Besides the money we'll save, the health benefits are priceless.

3. **Time:** Watching television, especially NFL football, was my way to decompress after a hard day at work. (Jonathan tells me he watched NHL hockey regularly for half a century but finally stopped a few years ago.) Over the years, it's surprising just how much time is wasted watching mindless TV (whether sports, reality TV, game shows or much of the other drivel that passes for "entertainment" on the tube). When you add social media (e.g., Facebook, Twitter, Snapchat) the numbers are frightening.

There is only so much time in the day and to waste a major portion of it on non-productive activities doesn't make a lot of sense. TV is the easy choice, the path of least resistance for many of us. Do what I have done and replace the TV/Internet habit with reading and exercising more. Through watching TV we fill our minds with so many negative things, and now I feel much more positive about things. Not a bad trade-off!

Of course, we're all different: Jonathan has always been a big reader but finds that after a long day of reading and writing, the last hour of the evening can be devoted to watching quality TV shows like those that air on *Masterpiece Theatre* Sunday nights on PBS, or programs of similar quality on the BBC, the CBC, or the Australian Broadcasting Corporation. The emphasis is on the word *quality*: if that's present, Jonathan feels that an hour of TV in moderation makes for a good transition between processing information and sleep.

HABITS AND THE POWER OF COMPOUNDING

Compound interest is the eighth wonder of the world. He who understands it, earns it. He who doesn't, pays it.
—*Albert Einstein*

Ask your financial adviser about the most important rule to follow in order to grow wealth, and she or he will undoubtedly talk about the power of compounding and diversification. When you put the power of compounding to work for you, your money will grow at exponential rates. That's the positive side, but the power of compounding can also work against you.

Even a harmless little habit, such as going to Starbucks or Tim Hortons every morning, can translate into big money thanks to the magic of compounding. For example, Mike has developed the habit of visiting Tim's most days, and he spends at least $5 every time. If instead of spending this $5 he had invested it at a 6 per cent return, over the course of twenty years he would end up saving close to $70,000. In other words, that daily Tim's run will end up costing Mike $70,000. Is the coffee at Tim's really that good? Wouldn't Mike be much better off just making his own coffee and toast at home?

Cutting back on visits to the coffee shop is just one example of how we can take action to reduce the "habit interest" that costs us a lot of money over time. Other examples are your cable bill, cell phone bill, Internet bill, buying books frequently instead of going to a library, and even activities that are as destructive to your health as to your pocketbook, cigarettes being the obvious example.

Every time you eliminate frivolous expenses, the power of compounding will eventually turn every penny saved into nickels, and if invested properly over the long run, the nickels will grow into dimes, quarters and so on. The thing to understand is that if you do something small repeatedly, the benefits or costs will accrue exponentially over time. Whether that effect is negative or positive is based on choices we make every day.

This rule applies outside finance too. Let's use health as an example. Mr. A is a successful executive who works hard but is so stressed out at the end of the day that he needs to decompress by sitting in front of the TV for the evening, munching on potato chips and enjoying a beer or three. By contrast, Mr. B has a similar job, but he decompresses by going to the gym a few times a week. He also goes for a nice stroll with his wife after dinner each night. Now imagine whose shoes you would rather be in after twenty years of these habits. Here's a clue: we hope you didn't pick Mr. A because he might have died from a heart attack by then!

Victory Lap gives all of us a chance to write our own story. We need to be intentional with the rest of our lives through goal setting and the adoption of good habits and routines. Solid financial and lifestyle habits should be based on an understanding of what will happen in the long term because of them. If we change our bad habits, we can change our future and improve our chances for a much happier ending. Identify those little habits that are holding you back and replace them with good ones. Always remember that tiny successes achieved each day will compound into large successes over time.

Time as a Resource

Every Day Matters

Time is more valuable than money. You can get more money, but you cannot get more time.
    —*Jim Rohn*

Achieving Findependence means you have earned the freedom (time) to spend your days as you please. This is potentially liberating, but you have to ensure that you don't waste time; it is all too fleeting and you will one day realize that a shortage of time will start to eliminate opportunities rather than create new ones. Eventually your physical abilities, and ultimately your mental faculties, will start to diminish and your options will begin to narrow. The key is to recognize time for what it is, so you can maximize its use and avoid any regrets down the road.

The good news is that if you were able to juggle your time and priorities successfully when you were in the Corp, it should be a snap to achieve a satisfying work–life balance once you start

After losing his keys, Jonathan had to be more careful about how he used his time.

your Victory Lap. Remember, you have the same twenty-four hours per day that Bill Gates, Warren Buffett, Prem Watsa, Ian Telfer, and Mark Zuckerberg have. How do you plan on spending yours? The most important decision you make each day is how you will invest your time. There's a Mark Twain quotation we refer to later in the book, and it's fitting to mention here also: "Twenty years from now you will be more disappointed by the things you didn't do than by the things you did do."

By effectively managing your time in Victory Lap you can create one of the most fulfilling and inspiring periods of your life. The freedom you'll experience in this unique phase will allow you to customize a work–life balance that works specifically for you. And soon you'll come to realize that, yes, you can have it all!

TIME, MONEY, AND LIFE ENERGY

One thing you discover early in the experience of a Victory Lap is the fluidity of time and its continued connection to money. It's a common observation that "time is money," but the corollary is also valid: "Money is time."

During the years of working toward financial independence, you are trading time for money, which amounts to transforming your human capital into financial capital that can be used in the distant future. As we all know, a young person just entering the workforce has potentially millions of dollars' worth of *human* capital ready to deploy but very little in the way of *financial* capital.

As the decades progress toward Findependence, this human capital starts to decrease, even as financial capital grows. In the old construct called full-stop retirement, the ultimate aim was to have enough financial capital in old age that it would no longer be necessary to use any of your human capital to generate money. No matter how you envision your retirement years, you just can't count indefinitely on your human capital to be available to convert into wealth. That's why the financial institutions are constantly nagging us to save for retirement.

Closely connected to the concepts of human capital, financial capital, time, and money is the idea of life energy. We all have a certain amount of spiritual essence or life force. When we take on a physical or mental task, some of this energy is expended, and we know, too, that we eat and sleep to recharge this energy. Like our time, it appears that our life energy is also a finite resource.

One of the classic books on financial independence is devoted to the interplay between life energy and money: *Your Money or Your Life: Transforming Your Relationship with Money and Achieving Financial Independence*, by Joe Dominguez and Vicki Robin. Dominguez retired from Wall Street at age thirty-one and never again accepted money for any work he did.

A key concept in the book is that money is something for which we choose to trade our life energy. Every time you deploy life energy (part of which is your time) on a money-creating task, realize that you have that much less life energy left for the future. Life energy is precious because it is finite and, once expended, is gone forever. If the task you performed resulted in payment in the form of money, you need to view that money as, in essence, a tiny portion of your personal life energy.

Of course, life energy can be expended on other things than generating money, even though full-time jobs in our primary careers do tend to consume about one-third of our waking time (and a lot of our life energy). Life energy is also expended on non–money-generating activities, such as cultivating relationships with family and friends, volunteering in the community, and purely "fun" leisure activities that are more apt to consume amounts of money rather than bring in money.

Charles Sharun is a friend of ours whose day job was as a painter of sets in the film business. He moved to the country in his late sixties in order to pursue his dream of becoming a full-time artist. But even before he made the move, he would build small stakes in the lucrative film business, then take chunks of time off in order to focus on his dream. Charles calls this "buying time." By working hard for six months at a time on one or two major film projects, in return he was able to save up enough money to "buy" six months of precious time to devote to his art.

Looking at it from this perspective, money is precious, assuming you agree that your life energy is also precious. So when it comes time to spend the money, you need to view its possible expenditure as the equivalent of dissipating your personal life energy. It's fine if the expenditure is a worthwhile one: either a cherished life experience (e.g., travel, education, time with family) or an item of consumption that enhances your physical well-being (e.g., nutritious food, smart clothes that make you employable, a roof over your head). But the flip side of spending money, and hence expending some of your life energy, comes when you in essence "waste" that money. We've all done so at some point in our lives: perhaps buying an exercise bike that never gets used beyond being a handy place to throw your clothes, blowing money at a casino, or taking a flyer on a speculative penny stock or a so-called blue chip like Nortel that promptly falls to zero. In all these cases, you end up with nothing to show for your expenditure of money and, therefore, nothing to show for the life energy you spent to accumulate that money. You have "wasted" not just your time but also your limited life energy and the money into which that time and energy was transformed.

THERE'S REALLY ONLY ONE DAY: DON'T WASTE IT

If you believe that life energy is precious, then so is the time you have available to expend life energy. When we enter this life, we're all given the same deal: each day we live has only twenty-four hours, and not even a billionaire can turn that twenty-four hours into one hour more. Henry Blodget once devoted his column at *Business Insider* to this very topic. He noted that most humans get about seventy-five years of existence on this planet, which translates into 3,900 weeks, the equivalent of approximately 27,000 days, or 648,000 hours.

When we saw that number—648,000 hours—we were astonished. That's not a lot of time, and it's a remarkably finite figure. Those of us fortunate enough to accumulate $648,000 probably don't view such a sum of money as infinite; we're well aware of how fast it could be depleted over a long retirement. So isn't the amount of 648,000 hours just as finite?

Suddenly, those sixteen hours of the twenty-four-hour day that we call "waking time" become even more precious. In each week, you have a total of 168 hours—only 112 if you consider that you "lose," on average, fifty-six hours to sleeping. Blodget observed that 150 years ago, seventy of those 112 waking hours were spent working. Today, thanks to the productivity-enhancing effects of technology, the average workweek in most countries has dropped by about thirty hours. Sadly, and this has profound implications for our Victory Lap concept, we spend most of that extra time watching television. According to research done by The Nielsen Company, Americans spend on average a whopping four hours a day watching TV, or twenty-eight hours a week.

A follow-up to Blodget's column was done by *Business Insider*'s Andy Kiersz in mid-2015, and he found slightly different statistics from the 2014 American Time Use survey. Based on that information, sleep continues to account for the biggest slice of the day: 8.8 hours on average, or eight hours and forty-eight minutes. When it came to work and work-related activities, because the survey participants included the unemployed or "retired," who would have spent zero hours a day working, this brought down the overall average and offset the normal eight hours that most full-time workers spend, but these activities still came second, accounting for an average of 3.59 hours. We'll round it up to four working hours, which is pretty significant. Watching TV accounted for 2.82 hours a day, while household activities made up 1.77 hours, leisure activities (other than watching TV) 1.48 hours and—get this—eating and drinking accounted for 1.17 hours. Personal care or grooming was 0.78 hours, educational activities were a tiny 0.42 hours a day, and exercise was an even tinier 0.29 hours.

To get a reality check on how limited our hours are on this planet, we recommend you watch a three-minute video on

YouTube that really brings the point home: https://www.youtube.
com/watch?v=BOksW_NabEk. Or just google "You have 28,835
days. Here's how you will spend them." The video shows 28,835
jelly beans, each one signifying a day of your life. Of course, the
fortunate will have more than 28,835 days in their lives; the unfortunate will have less, but 28,835 is the average on which the
video is based.

Our main premise—and we'll concede it's a mental concept,
albeit a useful one—is that "There's only one day." If you accept
this, it follows that every day matters and should not be squandered. For most human beings the day consists of sixteen hours,
the other eight being given over to sleep. We acknowledge that
there are some who extract eighteen or twenty hours or more
of productivity in their day by going with less sleep, but for the
purpose of argument, let's agree on a sixteen-hour day. Now
consider that everything you see on earth, from the pyramids
to the CN Tower, the greatest corporation, the longest novel,
and the most stirring symphony was created by human beings
in a series of sixteen-hour days, or more likely eight- or nine-
hour days. Yes, big projects require the stringing together of
hundreds or perhaps thousands of days, but the basic unit is
the single day. That day has a structure that is replicated over
weeks, months, and years.

For an office worker, the structure of a single working day is
very familiar. While there may be various internal and external
meetings on different days so that, superficially, each day will
appear somewhat unique, in a given week Monday, Tuesday,
Wednesday, Thursday, and Friday will unfold in pretty much the
same way for the worker: waking at a certain hour, commuting
to the office to arrive by 9 a.m., experiencing a whir of activity
or meetings followed by lunch, experiencing another whir until
about 5 p.m., then commuting home, and so it goes.

When you leave the structure of the office workday for Victory Lap Retirement, your success or failure during this stage will depend largely on how you approach the structure of the basic template for every day. The key to creating an effective template for your typical day is to recognize how mental and physical energy ebbs and flows over the day, and to build that into a structure for the model day that works for you.

HOW TO WORK JUST FOUR HOURS A DAY

If there's one thing Victory Lap provides, it's time freedom. No longer shackled to the eight-hour day of the Corp, you're free to practice something called "the four-hour workday." As you'll see, it's also possible to adapt this concept while you're still in the Corp: you can build a high-intensity four-hour day into the average eight-hour day, and that day can be repeated over and over again, with variations and accommodations that adapt to particular changing circumstances.

The idea for the four-hour workday originated in the 1950s, when William J. Reilly wrote a book called *How to Make Your Living in Four Hours a Day Without Feeling Guilty About It*. Reilly pointed out that when you look at very highly creative people, such as composers, novelists, or even high-level executives, they really have only four or five hours of high-level mental energy available daily to perform the tasks they have to do, and very few general types of workers expend high energy for every hour of their eight-hour workday.

For senior managers and creative types, what's important is the high-level brainpower being expended, not the amount of time one's bum adheres to an office chair. So it's important, whether you're a salesperson, executive, artist, musician, or writer to spend at least two hours of the workday morning doing the work you're really paid for: making cold calls or closing deals if you're in sales, writing articles if you're a writer, writing a symphony if you're a composer, and so on. Having done your two-hour morning stint, you're then free to spend two hours over lunch networking, learning, or exercising, as long as you promise yourself to spend at least two hours in the afternoon doing the work you're really paid to do.

Of course, most corporations like to see plenty of face time from their employees, preferably from 9 to 5. And so, if you're still in the Corp you may have to resort to a compromise, which is a four-hour day tucked inside the eight-hour office day. As an example, imagine that your morning shift of "real work" is between 10 a.m. and noon and that the afternoon shift between 2 and 4 p.m. involves being at your desk making sales calls, editing, writing, budgeting, or whatever. Note that this leaves an hour both first thing in the morning and at the end of the day for doing things like reading the paper, dealing with email, or checking social media. It's perfectly fine to "gear up" in the first hour or two of the corporate day and "wind down" toward the end, just so long as you get the "real" four hours of high-level brain activity done. It's that activity, after all, for which you're getting paid the big bucks.

If you absorb these concepts and start practicing them, you may catch yourself at odd moments saying to yourself, "There's only one day." Hopefully it will add some zest to the particular day you are experiencing or even increase your sense of urgency or appreciation of the moment. We need to relish the power of the present moment because that's the only time that's under our control. Making the most of your Victory Lap means making the most of each day you've been gifted to experience.

The corollary of "There's only one day" is "Every day matters." No matter how large the tasks are before you, you can only tackle them one day at a time. If you deploy your life energy on the important tasks each and every day, you can be sure your goals will be achieved. You know what they say about how you eat an elephant: one bite at a time. Waste a precious day of what we call "Monday to Friday time," and you've lost a bit of momentum.

Some may point out that the measurement of time can be arbitrary and argue that there's essentially only this second or this hour—or only the Now, as Eckhart Tolle expounds in his book *The Power of Now: A Guide to Spiritual Enlightenment.* What we're arguing here is that the day (the one day) is the fundamental unit of time that rules our lives. Our universe has been so constructed that our earth takes a trajectory through the heavens in such a fashion that the nearest star—the sun—appears to rise in the morning and to set in the evening. When we can see it, the moon comes out after sunset, and the stars make themselves visible, signalling the end of another day. So yes, a day *is* special and when you think about it, there's only one day, endlessly repeated with subtle variations.

Going back to the YouTube jelly bean video, we are creatures assigned 20,000 or 30,000 days on this planet, with each of those days made up of twenty-four hours, no more no less. The hour allotted to the billionaire is no longer than the hour experienced by a panhandler. How you choose to spend those twenty-four hours makes all the difference in your life.

MAKE THE MOST OF EVERY DAY IN YOUR VICTORY LAP

As any financial planner can tell you, if you knew precisely the date of your demise, it would be a simple matter to calculate how much money you could safely withdraw from your portfolios each year during retirement. You wouldn't have to worry about when your money would run out because you'd plan for it to run out a few days after you were buried. You know the old joke: The last cheque you should write should be to your undertaker, and it should bounce! Of course, being the considerate person that you are, in actual fact you would arrange a prepaid funeral to spare your heirs the expense.

Unfortunately (or perhaps fortunately, depending how you look at it), we generally do *not* have advance knowledge of our death day. We all hope it's thirty or forty or more years from now, but of course it's quite possible that today will turn out to be our last day. This is why there's some wisdom in the saying that we should live as if every day is our last day on earth, because one day it will be. This is another reason that we are inspired to adapt the *Three Boxes of Life* concept so that you can incorporate at least an hour or two of leisure, learning, and satisfying work into each day. This is easier to achieve in your Victory Lap than at any other time in your life. This special period allows you to achieve the kind of balance in your life that you can only dream about during any other time.

Think how sad it would be to spend your youth entirely at school learning and your middle years entirely at work, and then die prematurely just as your golden years of leisure were about to begin. Tragically, we see this all the time: money-oriented top executives or entrepreneurs who work around the clock in the sole pursuit of a large sum of money that will supposedly enable them to move from 100 per cent work mode to 100 per cent leisure mode at the right moment. It's largely a pipe dream and the basis for the popular saying (usually by those not so driven), "I don't want to be the richest man in the cemetery."

It's far better, we think, to mix up the boxes a bit so that they're non-sequential in your life and spread more evenly throughout your lifespan. That is, taking a Victory Lap allows you to play a little more in your earning years (taking some of your retirement time a little early). Victory Lap also lets you work a little in your life beyond full-time employment, earning a little "fun" money while keeping you more stimulated, challenged, and active than a life of unending leisure would do. Taking a Victory Lap can introduce more balance into your life not only each and every day that you are running that Victory Lap, living a new kind of retirement, but also throughout your life, as you redistribute your work, leisure, and retirement time.

Lastly, whether you are employed full-time or not, we also like the idea of flipping the three boxes around so that instead of stretching over a fifty-year span of life (or more) they stretch over a single day: the day that you will repeat, with variations, thousands of times over your life. And with it you will benefit from thousands of hours of learning, earning, and leisure, all experienced in the now of each day, the only day there really is.

9

Health Is Wealth

If I knew I was going to live this long I would have taken better care of myself.
    —Eubie Blake

Given the financial focus of this book, you might think the number-one worry of retirees is outliving their money. While that is certainly a major concern, surprisingly, it appears that the single biggest fear is deteriorating health. This is perfectly rational. Good health offers a freedom few people appreciate until they no longer have it. Health is one of those things we tend to take for granted until suddenly life takes a turn for the unexpected and health suddenly becomes an issue.

To ignore one's health in the single-minded pursuit of money or, worse, to abuse one's body in the pursuit of wealth is frankly a foolish proposition. If you break through the Findependence finish line with oodles of cash and an enormous investment portfolio, it will be a Pyrrhic victory if that financial wealth comes at the expense of your physical or mental well-being, or indeed your relationships.

Perhaps it's more than just a coincidence that the terms health and wealth are practically homonyms (they sound the same, save for a different letter at the beginning of each word). We'd go so far as to say that health *is* wealth, but not the reverse; we don't believe that wealth is health. Just ask any multi-millionaire who's on death's door. All the cash in the world can't buy back health that has been lost. You can't put a price on health. You may not perceive your present vibrant health as an asset, but you'll surely realize it as that if you suddenly lose it. Remember our earlier discussion on human capital: human capital presumes a healthy body and mind that is able to convert that capital into financial capital.

The good news is that Victory Lap is a holistic concept that spans the whole spectrum of the post-corporate lifestyle. It's as much about health as it is about wealth, which means that when planning your Victory Lap you must ensure that it includes exercise, proper diet, relationships, and—as chapter 10 will explore—the spiritual dimension.

As this book neared completion, Mike's mother was residing in a nursing home. Spending time visiting her there, Mike was able to observe first-hand the many benefits of having good health by observing so many people who have so little of it. It really hit home for him that without good health it doesn't matter how large your investment portfolio is. We spend so much time and energy saving and worrying about whether we will have enough money for retirement; but the reality is that if physically you can't get out of bed, does it really matter what you can afford to spend your money on? The truth is that if you cannot meet the physical demands of the adventures you've dreamt about and saved for, you are just as poor as the person who didn't save and can't afford to go on those adventures.

It was these kinds of considerations that prompted Jonathan's subtitle for *Findependence Day* and the tagline for the Hub: achieving financial independence "while you're still young enough to enjoy it." Sure, a common response to financial insecurity is to "just keep working," but can you really count on perfect health well into your sixties or your seventies?

Those visits to the nursing home served as a wake-up call when Mike realized it's only a matter of time before we all succumb to stroke, heart attack, cancer, Parkinson's, Alzheimer's or other forms of dementia, or some other age-related illness. But he also knows we can increase the odds of enjoying more quality years if we keep our bodies fit, our minds challenged, and our hearts engaged. Your Victory Lap is a special time in your life that affords you the time, money, flexibility, and vitality to do all of those things. This is a time to take care of you all-around, and to live life to the fullest on all fronts. As a result you may just find that the Victory Lap years are the richest, happiest, and most rewarding time of your life.

PLAN TO BE HEALTHY

Each of us has the power to improve our health so we can continue to do the things we love today for many years to come. In the end it's all about personal choices we make regarding activity, involvement, and attitude.

Generally speaking, over the years baby boomers have learned to take better care of their minds and bodies than the generations that preceded them. They tend to eat more sensibly and most are well aware of the value of regular exercise. Indeed, the trend to healthier eating is apparent in the North American restaurant business. While fast food chains like McDonald's and Burger King stagnate in the stock market, there is a whole new wave of companies that cater to healthy eating and healthy living: Chipotle, Whole Foods, White Wave, Hain Celestial, to name four publicly traded U.S. stocks. Meanwhile, makers of coloured, sweetened water—Coca-Cola and Pepsi—are scrambling to move their product lines to more healthy choices in beverages or snacks.

The boomer generation has a narrow window left in which to travel and enjoy other pursuits before their possibilities are curtailed by health issues. On average, people will make it only to age sixty-seven without some form of disability that will moderately or severely limit them. Data from Statistics Canada show there is a one-in-three chance of someone in the 65–74 age bracket being disabled, which means not being able to work or move about freely. In fact, people are more likely to become disabled than to die prematurely. The bottom line is that disease is unpredictable and you need to enjoy life while you still can. Hence the aforementioned slogan about achieving Findependence "while you're still young enough to enjoy it!"

Medical issues that prevent people from working are wide-ranging and often caused by being stressed out and over-extended by work and other responsibilities. This can lead to debilitating conditions like depression and anxiety. On the physical side, those who are overweight are more likely to develop type 2 diabetes and be vulnerable to related complications like heart disease or stroke. Well-being guru Dr. Lesley Horton blames our increasingly sedentary lifestyles and poor diets for the fact that roughly one-quarter of the population is considered obese. This is the idle generation: many already sport pot bellies, "muffin tops," and double chins. Those who exhibit these visual signals have a heightened risk for cancers and other serious diseases. There is even a new term—diabesity—which refers to being afflicted with both diabetes and obesity.

Upon leaving the Corp, some may choose to buy a comfy La-Z-Boy chair, upgrade the cable package, or binge-watch *30 Rock* reruns on Netflix. But by spending most of your time sitting around munching on snack foods, sooner or later your health will pay a steep price. Why act older than you really are? Smart people realize that to have a high quality of life they must challenge themselves every day. You can't just settle in and kill time, waiting for the end. You need to take an interest in yourself and extract every ounce of life's possibilities. Make the decision to thrive, not just survive!

LIFE EXPECTANCY AND LONGEVITY

A big theme in this book is that of extended longevity, not just for the baby boomers but also for their children—the millennials and/or Generation X. We believe the combination of an exercise

regime, healthy eating, and continued breakthroughs in medical science and biotechnology means people are going to live a lot longer than we once might have imagined. Therefore, our primary careers may last a good long time, and it also means we have time to plan properly for a well-rounded Victory Lap, one that could last anywhere from one to three or more decades.

Traditionally, financial planners have pencilled in ninety as a target age for making an investment portfolio last. Obviously, some will die before that age and others will die after it. Spend some time reading the obituary pages of any newspaper and you will witness the trend toward rising life expectancies. While disease, accident, and sheer bad luck may take us off the stage in our forties or fifties, or even before that, there are plenty of centenarians breaking past age 100 and even a fair number who make it to 105. While the oldest recorded human in modern history is France's Jeanne Calment (who reached 122), it's not hard to imagine some of the millennial cohort living beyond that age, perhaps to 125 or, as some predict, even age 150.

We suggest that when conducting your financial planning you ask your financial adviser to work out a "what if?" scenario for you by adding ten years to your expected lifespan. If, for example, you always figured you'd keel over at eighty-five, readjust your thinking and imagine living to age ninety-five. How will that affect your planning, your retirement date, and your financial projections?

EXTEND YOUR WORKSPAN *AND* YOUR FUNSPAN

It's one thing if your "bonus" years afforded by breakthroughs in longevity are spent in declining health, but entirely another if you also gain extra vibrant, healthy years. If healthy living and eating, and avoiding harmful habits like excess consumption of drugs, alcohol, or tobacco do grant you some extra years of life, it's likely that most of those years will be healthy and potentially productive ones.

If your what-if exercise of tacking on ten more years to your life expectancy opens your eyes to the possibilities, we would suggest splitting the difference: allocate five of those extra years to work (your "workspan") and another five to leisure, or what we call your "funspan." After all, is it not logical that if you are going to have an extended *lifespan*, you also have an extended *workspan*? The fact is that you will more than likely need to continue working longer than you may have planned just to finance that longer life you'll live. So, for example, if you once believed you would "retire" at sixty-two and live to eighty-five, try to imagine you and your spouse living to ninety-five. Take half the extra ten years and assign them to your workspan, meaning that you now plan to work in some fashion or another until age sixty-seven instead of age sixty-two.

This does not have to be more years in the corporate cubicle, though of course if you're in a congenial workplace you might actually want to stay there. There are huge financial advantages to staying in the company pension plan an extra five years as you also let your investment portfolio grow for another half decade and delay the receipt of government benefits like Social Security or the Canada Pension Plan.

But if you had your heart set on stepping off the corporate hamster wheel by age sixty-two, you can still do that without embracing a full-stop retirement. This may be the time to implement your own version of a Victory Lap: start your own business; create a website; reinvent yourself to become a novelist, painter, stand-up comic, or public speaker; go back to school to study theology; enrol in medical school; become a lawyer—whatever your long-suppressed dream may be. Or maybe you'll do something you had never contemplated in your youth but now realize may be perfect for you in your Victory Lap incarnation.

NEVER STOP LEARNING

At some point, extended physical health may mean the long-term threat is no longer to your body but to your mind. The older you get and the longer you live, the greater the odds are that you or your partner may be attacked by the twenty-first century scourge of dementia, and in particular Alzheimer's disease, which is having an increasing presence in the lives of North Americans, including in our popular culture. One such example is the novel and film *Still Alice*, which vividly portrays the plight of a university linguistics professor who suffers from early-onset Alzheimer's. While the cause may be genetic in only a small number of cases, this is another area where scientific research is pushing the boundaries. Even as we write these words, there are press reports of increasingly hopeful research coming from academics striving to lessen the increasing prevalence of Alzheimer's.

In the meantime, just as we have learned to take care of our bodies by eating well and exercising, we should take the trouble to keep the brain limber and active. To us, the brain is a muscle that needs to get a daily mental workout. This is one reason we believe in encore careers even for those who leave the corporate world. The workplace provides both mental and social stimulation that has to be a positive for the brain. Just having a sense of purpose every morning when you awake is a good reason for continuing to stay active in the workplace, if only on a part-time basis.

But even if you embrace a "full-stop" retirement by your mid-sixties, eschewing paid work of any kind, you still should never stop learning. Take night-school courses at a nearby college or university. Learn a new musical instrument. One of our friends took up the clarinet after taking early retirement in her mid-fifties, for example. We know a former financial adviser of the same age who was counselled by a life coach (his sister-in-law) and finally revived a childhood dream of becoming an actor. Today, he has an agent, has appeared on the silver screen in a film short, is active making TV commercials, and is well on the way to creating his own theatrical productions.

Entire books describe how to keep the brain active and keep dementia at bay for as long as possible. Perhaps you had a childhood passion for a game like chess that you can rediscover. You can play chess with anyone in the world at any time by playing online, and bridge players can do the same. Others will like to play Sudoku in the daily newspaper. It doesn't really matter which of these activities you choose; the point is to emulate the fictional detective Hercule Poirot and keep "those little grey cells" active.

THE POWER OF A POSITIVE ATTITUDE

An extraterrestrial visitor to twenty-first century North America would no doubt be baffled by what it observed of the privileged citizens of the United States and Canada. Despite all our wealth, labour-saving devices, and technological marvels, very few of us are truly happy. We distract ourselves with alcohol, drugs, television, gambling, shopping, and so much more. More people die by their own hand than are murdered. We are much better off today than at any other time in history, but surveys confirm that most employees are unhappy at their jobs, with depression rates getting higher year over year. Something is seriously out of whack.

The apparent explanation is that we live in an increasingly stressful and negative world and most of us just don't know how to deal with it. People naturally tend to focus on the negative, and of course the news media tend to emphasize whatever is going badly in the world. As journalists quip about news judgement, "If it bleeds, it leads." Terrorism and the 24/7 news cycle tend to leave even the most optimistic among us somewhat anxious about the future. Add in economic and financial insecurity, and it's little wonder that even affluent North Americans worry about the future.

Those of you still accumulating wealth may wonder why seemingly "rich" folk often keep working. We can tell you that those with large portfolios of cash and bonds worry about minuscule interest rates, while those with large portfolios of stocks or equity funds worry about another crash in the stock market. If anything, those with lots of money tend to worry about it more than those who do not. Over time, what goes into our minds, the experiences we have had, and what we flood our minds with becomes our reality. We become what we think about all day long. Therefore, having a pessimistic attitude will make you susceptible to depression, higher stress levels, and poor health. Odds

are that unless you take proactive measures to counteract this negative mindset, it will result in a shorter lifespan.

You can adopt a positive attitude about life or you can choose to remain on the dark side. You can make a conscious decision to focus on the positive and filter and control what goes into your mind. You can reduce your mind's exposure to violent television shows or movies and negative people who constantly moan and complain, and instead train your mind how to focus on the positive and the hopeful possibilities in every situation. Try to surround yourself with successful, positive people who will serve as a good role model and encourage you to chase your dreams. Look forward to each new day just like you did when you were younger, with an attitude of joy and wonder. Life is wonderful if you look at it the right way.

A happy corollary of this is that optimists tend to do better in business, whether they are working for someone else or running their own business. So if you plan to be an entrepreneur during your Victory Lap, you'd be well advised to think like an optimist, if you don't already! If you're an investor, focusing on the positive is more likely to permit you to enjoy good investment returns. As any financial adviser will tell you, in the long run you will make higher returns with stocks than bonds and cash, but to buy and hold stocks, you need to have a certain amount of faith and confidence in the future. Generally, that faith will pay off if you're disciplined enough to invest for the long run.

Instead of fretting about all the bad things that can happen, focus on what you want in your life and be grateful for all the things that you already have. Optimism *can* be learned, as positive psychology guru Martin Seligman reminds us in his book *Learned Optimism: How to Change Your Mind and Your Life*. Or read Shawn Achor's book *The Happiness Advantage: The Seven Principles of Positive Psychology that Fuel Success and Performance at Work*, which presents a useful paradigm shift: happiness is not something that can be deferred until after you succeed in life; be happy here and now and that positive attitude will contribute to your eventual success.

Remember that, as in the dictionary, happiness comes *before* success! Too many of us place happiness at the back of the bus. Why do we tend to defer happiness and push it further out? We delude ourselves that we will be happy once we pay off the mortgage. Or after we save another $500,000 for retirement. Why can't we just be happy now?

The answer is that you can find ways to be happy now (read or reread the story of the Mexican fisherman at the end of the next chapter). The truth is that being happy means you are more positive. When you are positive you are sharper, have more energy, and are more motivated to accomplish your goals. Try to remove your focus on money and accumulating a certain level of capital by a certain date; instead, relax and start living again—just like the Mexican fisherman. Don't compete with others or be tempted to keep up with the proverbial Joneses. It's hard not to feel envious when you see your friends or neighbours driving expensive cars, living in monster homes, and going on expensive vacations. But if you remember to practice gratitude, it will help your attitude immensely.

When you're running a Victory Lap, instead of being competitive (as in the corporate world) you need to think in terms of self-improvement. Competitiveness means competing with *others*, while self-improvement is about competing with *yourself*. It's very hard to get competitiveness out of our blood, as many have been in that environment all their working lives. Who hasn't had to endure sales contests and quotas or grade fellow workers on a bell curve that permits only a tiny minority to "exceed expectations" on performance reviews? Business leaders seem to have created an environment in which we always have to beat the other guy or gal. It's like we're all Roman gladiators doing battle in the Colosseum.

Most of us were taught to chase the money, and even in the Victory Lap (as we can both attest) it can prove hard to get away from that mindset. Instead of thinking about money all the time (as a payback for your time), think about how good you will feel when you help someone, and try to have fun whether or not you can cut an invoice at the end of the activity.

In short:

- Have a good attitude, be a positive person, and try to make at least one person smile every day.
- Have a sense of humour and laugh every day.
- Develop an attitude of "If they can do it, I can do it."

Go back to having a beginner's mindset about life, similar to how a child views the world. Be curious and keep growing because of that curiosity.

Aging Is a Matter of Attitude

Your attitude determines how you approach life and how you experience it. You can only accomplish what you *think* you can achieve. You likely can recall the children's story about the "little train that could," or how some people believe they can do an Ironman triathlon because the approach they take to goal-setting is, "Anything is possible if you want it badly enough." What we do and what we are depends on what we think.

Today you are where your attitude has *brought* you, while your future is where your attitude will *take* you. Even aging is largely a matter of attitude. You can be seventy-five and still act like you are forty-five; or you may be only forty-five chronologically yet be perceived as acting like you're seventy-five. Refuse to be defined by age. Optimists live longer than pessimists, and this alone can add up to an extra seven-and-a-half years, on average.

Successful aging is about having a positive attitude toward aging. It's about having something exciting to look forward to and knowing what it takes to keep going mentally and physically, challenging yourself every day. No pain, no gain. This is partly what doing a Victory Lap is all about. Staying engaged and active, possibly even continuing to work, will give you purpose, fulfillment, a sense of accomplishment, and just enough of the challenge you need to keep yourself vibrant. But try to make it fun. Laugh at yourself: You're like a kid again! Hang around positive people who are attempting the same things you are. Stay away from boring, negative people. With them, it's like trying to save a drowning person—they just might take you down with them!

Dwelling on your problems rather than your possibilities is not the way to go through life. See the half-empty glass for what it is: half-filled. Be a positive person and you'll be healthier and happier than the pessimists. It makes no sense worrying about past events or mistakes unless you want to experience them for a second time (or more).

Control Your Mind and Stay in the Moment

The secret of health for both mind and body is not to mourn for the past, worry about the future, or anticipate troubles, but to live in the present moment wisely and earnestly.
—Buddha

Most of us are so focused on the future that we don't realize the beauty of the moment. We tend to drift through our days, guided largely by habits and routines, not really listening to or noticing what is happening around us. We hear things but don't focus on what they really mean. When we are home our thoughts are focused on work issues; at the office our minds are focused on what is happening at home. We need to slow down and focus on the present moment, to enjoy what we are doing while we're doing it.

What you focus on will determine your destiny, so it's important to use self-discipline and focus on the good stuff. Stop taking life so seriously. Take the time to watch a beautiful sunset; hear the silence around you. Appreciate what is all around you and appreciate each moment to its fullest. This problem of always being in a hurry to get somewhere usually gets worse as we get older.

DON'T PURSUE HAPPINESS, DISCOVER IT

Our souls are not hungry for fame, comfort, wealth, or power
. . . Our souls are hungry for meaning, for the sense that we

have figured out how to live so that our lives matter, so that
the world will be at least a little bit different for our having
passed through it.
    —*Rabbi Harold Kushner*

Victory Lap Retirement allows us to change from a "surviving mentality" to a "thriving mentality." A happy Victory Lap
Retirement is not a commodity that can be bought in a store or
online: it needs to be well-thought-out and planned so that it is
the perfect lifestyle for you, unique to your needs, goals, and
situation.

For his part, the American motivational speaker Zig Ziglar
made a practice of trying to brighten the moods of strangers
through random acts of kindness each day. When you make
someone else smile you end up smiling too. The very act of giving to others makes you feel better as well. Give it a try and see
for yourself.

Happiness occurs when you understand that what you are
seeking isn't to be found outside of yourself. You can't buy it, bor-
row it, or even steal it. Happiness is already inside you, waiting to
be rediscovered. No matter how much you have in the bank, how
many toys you have, or how much you earn, none of it will make
you happier in and of itself.

If you know what must happen in order for you to be happy,
why don't you just do it? Most of us will be unable to answer this
question, as it's easy to get sidetracked: life gets in the way, bills
need to be paid, and we tend to let our dreams slip away and lose
hope for the future. When you eventually wake up and begin to
live your life intentionally (literally "on purpose"), you will discover there is no better feeling than when you do something that
you love; something that excites you and makes you realize that
your contribution matters.

All of us have been given clues as to our purpose during our lifetime. We need to go back, review the tapes, and figure out our unique strengths, skills, and talents. Remember what it is that gets you excited and what you are passionate about, then figure out how it all fits together and what you want to be so you can live up to your full potential.

If you didn't discover this during your primary career, you definitely want to take advantage of your Victory Lap to do so. Once you discover your true calling you will know exactly where you want to go and what you plan on doing when you get there. The key is to stay in alignment with your purpose, passion, and your mission. Once you figure out and align "who you are" with "what you were born to do," you can't lose!

Having purpose is great for the soul. It makes you feel good and gives you a reason to get out of bed in the morning (remember the power of *ikigai*?). You need to create a sense of purpose for your life after full-time employment. It's about challenge and fulfillment, finding the perfect combination of striving and accomplishment that comes from achieving a big goal. Without purpose, life is meaningless.

After leaving your primary career and entering the Victory Lap, you need to feel that you still matter, that you're not invisible to the world but are still contributing to society in some form. People become passionate when they can tap into things that really matter to them. A happy life requires a fair degree of passion. Without it, life is without meaning.

Remember, true wealth is health. Having a Victory Lap Retirement will enrich your life, but you need a healthy body to run the race. The fact that a well-executed Victory Lap will also provide you with additional income and a larger nest egg is a bonus, but remember that the real payoff is the purpose you will find for yourself and live by every day.

10

Spiritual Health

One thing you can't hide is when you're crippled inside.
—John Lennon

Closely related to physical and mental health are emotional and spiritual health. Even if your parents have blessed you with a flawless genetic heritage and a robust physical body, these will count for little if you abuse those gifts with destructive habits and practices.

To us, physical health flows from mental health, and mental health in turn flows from spiritual health. All the money in the world will be of little comfort if your spiritual life or mental outlook isn't healthy. Recent news stories about the affliction of "affluenza" affecting the offspring of rich parents should be a cautionary warning about this: abundant financial wealth is no substitute for a solid moral compass that all parents should pass on to their children.

There are many different spiritual practices that you can adopt to nourish your soul and contribute to your overall mental and physical health. Like your Victory Lap in general, your

Mike searched the world over for happiness and contentment, and finally discovered it was in his backyard the whole time.

spiritual practices should be customized to suit your own personal needs and preferences. The point is that in this stage of your life you are probably better positioned to focus on this aspect of your well-being than at any other time before.

FIRST, PUT YOUR FINDEPENDENCE INTO PRACTICE

The first practice we recommend focusing on is consciously acting like the findependent person that you are. But it's not as easy as you think. It may take some time before you can fully accept your hard-won findependent status and start acting like the financially free being you have worked so hard to become. You must psychologically and emotionally embrace your Findependence before you can translate it into actual behaviour that fully takes advantage of the freedom you have so long pursued. Making some space in your life to focus on your spiritual health can help you get into that findependent frame of mind.

As we saw a little earlier in the book, a big part of the Victory Lap/Findependence idea is your own attitude. Author Robert Gignac put it well in the title of his financial novel, *Rich is a State of Mind: Building Wealth and Happiness—A Blueprint*. We can similarly assert that "Findependence is a state of mind." It doesn't matter how big your retirement nest egg is if you don't think you have enough to step off the corporate treadmill.

Both of us know first-hand how hard it is to break the working habit upon crossing the finish line of financial independence. The law of inertia means that bodies already in motion tend to stay in motion, so the initial response to sudden financial freedom is often to keep pursuing dollars. In Jonathan's case, his first entire year after reaching Findependence was dedicated to the "just keep working" philosophy. Technically this wasn't absolutely necessary, as he was in the fortunate position of having no mortgage, no consumer debt, and enough money in the bank to take an extended sabbatical. And to top it all off, he was (and is) blessed by a wife who continued to work full-time. Mike's situation was similar.

In many ways, this impetus to keep working is perfectly understandable. Achieving true Findependence may take between twenty-five and forty years of practicing the good old Protestant work ethic, keeping one's nose to the grindstone of employment, and maintaining the frugal behaviour that makes Findependence possible. It takes a hard-working, hard-saving attitude to lay the foundation of financial freedom, and living your life according to this attitude can be a hard habit to break. In Jonathan's case, it wasn't until the end of June 2015—by which time this book project had begun in earnest—that he really started to experience the more relaxed mindset of "work because you *want* to not because you *have* to," truly embracing the part-time freelance lifestyle that he preached in *Findependence Day*. You can also call this the "Work Optional" stage.

Looking back, it's not hard to see why this happened. Jonathan had spent a quarter of a century drawing a regular salary from just two employers, both of whom became clients after he reached Findependence. No wonder it took him a year to actually enjoy a stretch of free time as well—the first time in ages that he had neither an employment contract nor a short-term contract to provide writing or other editorial services.

Running a Victory Lap is freedom, certainly, but it may not be quite the exhilarating feeling of liberation you may imagine you'd experience on receiving a gold watch on your sixty-fifth birthday at a traditional retirement party. How quickly you embrace your Findependence—and start living the lifestyle it allows—will vary with temperament, age, and family circumstances. If your spouse and friends are all still working, it may seem natural to continue to do so yourself. But recognize that, to a large extent, remaining on the money treadmill may by this point be largely a self-imposed activity. Work has a momentum of its own: after all, for many years it was an absolute necessity.

One discovers in the Victory Lap that work continues to be an important component of this new lifestyle. But instead of it being the master, now it is you who is master and work becomes your servant. When you look at how your hours can be spent once you have seemingly infinite free time, you soon discover there are natural time limits to many of the activities you may have fantasized about doing back when you were still on the corporate merry-go-round.

You can exercise two hours a day if you're so inclined, you can absorb the news media for three or four hours, you can read books at stretches of two or three hours, you can play games like bridge for two or three hours, and you can watch TV for two or three hours (although we believe passive activities like watching TV or movies ideally should be reserved for the evening hours and even then only for an hour or two). But you discover soon enough that about the only activities you can consistently perform for seven or eight hours a day are sleeping and work. Little wonder that during our working years, life is a pattern of one-third sleep, one-third work, and one-third leisure time. As we all know when still at the stage of the primary career, the latter third is precious time for which there are many competing demands: grooming, food preparation, shopping, yardwork, and various leisure or social activities.

Findependence frees up a lot of discretionary hours that can be spent on whatever your passion is. Subtract an hour or two of commuting time and get the eight-hour work part of the day down to four or five (see chapter 8) and you'll discover how many more extra hours and activities can be packed into the typical Victory Lap day. Some of that extra time can be devoted to charitable and philanthropic work in the community, some on your spiritual practices and, ideally, a lot more time with family and friends, especially the ones who need you.

Relishing the time, space, and flexibility you have worked so hard to achieve in your Victory Lap can take many forms, and you'll need to figure out which practices are best for you. But we're willing to bet that making room for some or all of these in your life will be good for your soul.

BUILD IN ELECTRONIC DOWNTIME

Taking care of your spiritual health can be as simple as "getting off the grid" from time to time. Here in the twenty-first century, we are blessed by technological gadgets and "devices" that can serve as marvelous productivity aids. Indeed, the millennial generation has been raised on the Internet, smartphones, and sharing services, and they seem lost without their devices. But there's a place and time for using these machines. Our consumer culture offers no end of distractions, from television to movies to social media, all of which compete for tiny slivers of our attention and thus our life energy.

In theory, it costs nothing, either in money or effort, to still the mind and filter out all external stimuli. But society offers so many distractions and demands on our attention that looking within is anything but easy for the average citizen of western industrial democracies.

One easy way to conserve your life energy, or win some of it back, is to build a little electronic downtime into your Victory Lap. Try to walk outside without a Fitbit, smartphone, or any other electronic devices. Instead of connecting with people you've never met through social media, see if you can boost your life energy by using some more of your time to connect with your inner self.

Establish at least one room in your home as an electronics-free zone, free from the lights and sounds of most of the other rooms. It's difficult these days, but ideally your bedroom should have a minimum of lights and screens, including TVs, computers, tablets, or cell phones. Exposure to digital device screens affects the quality and duration of your sleep because of how the light emitted from the screens interferes with the body's ability to produce melatonin. And so, the more screens are eliminated from the period leading up to your bedtime, the better your sleep will be.

Even ten minutes every morning of attempted meditation (more on this practice below) should yield some fruit in terms of peace of mind and equanimity. If a dedicated meditation room is not for you, perhaps a particular designated space could do double duty for reading, yoga, or other forms of exercise. These intro-spective pursuits are a subtle thing and may not be for everyone at a particular stage of life. But remember that once you're off the treadmill and have experienced a modicum of Findependence, you may be ready to entertain activities you rationalized you "never had the time for" while you were still spinning the corpo-rate hamster wheel.

A good substitute for those who find it difficult to look with-in is instead looking outside yourself by appreciating nature. Jonathan, for example, lives within fifty yards of Lake Ontario and not a day goes by without a walk or bike ride along the lake (or in the winter, ice skating near the lake). It's been said that the most positive brainwave activity can be generated by a nature walk and the simple act of appreciating nature and beauty. Let the blue tranquil calm of the lake or the quiet green cathedral of the forest reflect your mind at rest.

MINDFULNESS

In trying to get yourself into the Findependence mindset, you might consider incorporating mindfulness and mindfulness meditation. Whether you are working full-time or not, mindful-ness is a powerful tool for nurturing a positive attitude, honing your focus, and creating overall well-being. While meditation is generally practiced for ten or twenty minutes once or twice a day, mindfulness is something that can and should be practiced throughout the day (see also chapter 8, Time as a Resource).

One book we'd recommend is Maria Gonzalez and Graham Byron's book on equanimity and mindfulness, entitled *The Mindful Investor: How a Calm Mind Can Bring You Inner Peace and Financial Security.* (We could, of course, turn that descriptive sub-title on its head by observing that if you already possess financial security via Findependence, then financial security can bring you a calm mind and inner peace.)

Either way, mindfulness is all about maintaining a positive attitude and focusing on the present moment, not just during your more formal morning or evening meditation practice (more to come on that shortly). Whatever activity you are engaged in at any given time, try to "be" with that activity, including "work" tasks and money-making activities. Stay focused on the task at hand, trying not to let the mind be dragged into dwelling on the regrets of yesterday or the anxieties of tomorrow.

In the 1960s, the counterculture guru Ram Dass (formerly Harvard University's "acid" researcher, Richard Alpert) epitomized the requisite attitude with his famous classic book, *Be Here Now*. Whether you're still working full-time or have started to enjoy the more leisurely pace of the Victory Lap, you should always strive to make time to still the mind and reflect.

It may be easier to devote time to these activities during the classic full-stop retirement, when there are fewer excuses for failing to take the time to look deep inside one's soul. By its very nature, business (i.e., busyness) is a distraction that prevents us from discovering our true selves. Once work is no longer such a commanding part of our lives, there's no longer an excuse not to discover our true selves. This is a good thing, so embrace the opportunity.

Certainly, though, compared to the frantic years of one's primary career, the more balanced years of Victory Lap Retirement are more conducive to the kinds of spiritual practices we describe. While it would be lovely to spend forty-five minutes every morning and another forty-five minutes every evening in deep meditation, few of us will have that kind of time (or commitment), even in the Victory Lap. Just ten minutes every morning is better than no minutes at all, and if you're still working full-time, even five minutes can be beneficial. Start small, be open to trying it (there are various smartphone apps that can help with your breathing and related disciplines), and if you start to get results, you can increase the rate and frequency of your sessions. Or you can attempt to move on to dedicated time for meditation.

Try to train your consciousness to be aware of the present moment; to be free of regret about the past and free from worry about the future. So, for example, if you're eating some tasty food, focus on the taste and don't start thinking of what you'll do once you've finished eating. If you're talking to a friend, be with that person and really listen to what he or she is saying. If you're looking at a sunset over a lake, be with the sunset. Spiritual writer and meditation advocate Paul Brunton advocated experiencing both sunrises and sunsets, bookending every day with a spiritual, aesthetic appreciation of nature that far transcends the hubbub of commerce and the daily bad news.

START YOUR DAY RIGHT WITH MEDITATION

Earlier we introduced the idea that there's really only one day. It's helpful to start that day—every day—with some spiritual discipline. It's important to make time to escape the noise of the world, and when better to do that than immediately upon rising at the start of that day? There is something magical about the first few hours of the morning. Time seems to slow down and a deep sense of stillness and calm fills the air.

Each of us needs to make a daily commitment to spend time in a quiet place so we can restore clarity to our world and become centred again. During this time we need to reflect on who we really are, and remember what's important and what's not. We talked about the importance of living in the moment and of cultivating a positive attitude. Meditation helps us to achieve this state of mind, slowing us down and clearing our mind of distractions, allowing us to remember all the good things in our lives. In meditation we can hear our inner voice and reconnect with who we really are. Use meditation to empty the mind of all worries and negative thoughts. Instead, focus on the positive aspects of your life, what makes you truly happy. It's there, but often you are just too busy to be aware of it.

You can easily add meditation to your morning or evening routine (or prayer and meditation, if you accept the notion that prayer is speaking to the Almighty and that meditation is listening to the response). A morning or evening (or both) spent in meditation or contemplation can set you up for the whole day, helping you visualize and plan for it. Then at the end of the day you can look back and reflect on the experiences and lessons learned, the personalities you encountered, and the challenges that can be renewed the following day.

Over time you will begin to see things differently, new ideas and opportunities will appear, and you will find ways to make your dreams come true. Without dreams and something to look forward to, it's hard to find a reason to get out of bed every morning. Start to listen intentionally to your inner voice and intuitions, learn to trust them, and become aware of all the possibilities around you. Trust your inner self and listen to what it is trying to say to you, then create a path aligned with your goals and dreams. This is your personal Victory Lap customized to the unique individual that is you! Small daily steps over time will get you there.

Most of us have been in survival mode for too long. In Victory Lap you have a chance to once again gain control over your life. Now is the time to be intentional with your life. It is no longer okay to go through it just surviving, it's time to really live and enjoy everything life can offer.

JOIN A COMMUNITY OF SPIRITUAL SEEKERS

If you feel you lack the discipline to get started on these kinds of practices on your own, seek out groups that can act as your spiritual support group. Finding or rediscovering a community of fellow spiritual seekers may provide a double benefit—not just in facilitating your growing spiritual side, but also in connecting with a community of like-minded souls. This could be in the form of the traditional church, mosque, or synagogue whose attendees meet on Sundays (or in some cases, Saturdays), or it could be less formal organizations, like yoga or pilates groups, for example.

The latter are springing up just about everywhere, often located near the local organic food store. Try to take advantage of the low-cost introductory courses many offer to beginners; you can become acquainted with the different practices and instructors and find those closest to your temperament and lifestyle. At the same time, you will start to meet some of your neighbours who have a similar approach to life. Some yoga centres even have designated "soul coaches," so there's a lot more to these mind/body practices than just contorting the body into various poses!

If you're more community-minded, you may choose the path of helping others through volunteering or philanthropy, donating your time and energy to hospitals, food banks, service clubs, old-age homes, hospices, or any number of worthy organizations. In so doing, you may well discover the truth that in getting outside of "self" and devoting your energies to others, your own problems appear smaller.

Those who are more intellectually inclined may choose simply to read about philosophy and religion, although again one might find more stimulation by taking an extension course at a nearby university. The advantage of meeting others with similar interests will be a bonus, one that recent widows or widowers may well come to appreciate if they meet a special someone.

Part of keeping the mind active and never ceasing to learn is reading, although this is largely a solitary activity. The local library is one of the great bargains out there: you can order the books you want online and they will be held for you, to be picked up on your next visit. Or you can download free e-books or audio books through services like OverDrive.

We know a group of middle-aged women who have a rotating book club, with the members taking turns once a month to host a light dinner and sample the wine cellar. It's as much a social event as it is a literary one, but like many other activities mentioned in this chapter, it serves a dual function: keeping the brain active for solitary reading while also bringing together a community of like-minded individuals.

BOREDOM VERSUS STRESS

Earlier we talked about boredom being the elephant in the room in retirement. Much of the Victory Lap Retirement lifestyle is about taking advantage of the time flexibility conferred by financial independence. During the wealth accumulation years, stress is often our constant companion. Just holding down a full-time job, raising a family and keeping the home fires burning is enough to keep the average North American fully occupied for decades.

For many, boredom is something many couples *wish* they could experience. This is perhaps why the traditional advertising message of full retirement seems to appeal to many of us: we've been so stressed out working and raising families that the idea of doing nothing at all at the end seems quite alluring—until you actually get there. We know quite a few early retirees, some fortunate enough to have been pensioned off by their early or mid-fifties. After a few months of "doing nothing," most start looking for part-time work, going back to school, preparing for a new encore career, or contemplating creating a business.

The danger is that you can soon find yourself overcommitted even in a well-executed Victory Lap. There's a fine line between boredom and stress. For the most part, the full-time primary career and associated family life is mostly filled with stress, which is why we advocate stress-reduction practices like exercise, proper diet, and spiritual disciplines like yoga or meditation. By contrast, the classic full-stop, do-nothing retirement may be at the opposite extreme: not enough stress, and hence boredom, whether it comes soon or later.

The beauty of Victory Lap Retirement is that you can design it right from the get-go with the proper mix of work and leisure. And to do that, you may well need a team to coach you. We all know about financial advisers, accountants, tax lawyers, and the other professionals who can help you achieve financial independence. But equally, we may need the services of "softer" advisers: life coaches, soul coaches, personal trainers, and even consultants who are specialists in decluttering or organizing files and emails.

For us at least, Findependence establishes a financial foundation to take our private dreams to a new, higher level. For Jonathan, the original point of Findependence was to allow time to do creative projects like novels (*Findependence Day* being the first of these) or the non-fiction book you are now reading. *Victory Lap Retirement* does meet our criterion of a long-term creative project that hopefully will add to the world's literary stores in a way that will resonate with at least some readers.

THE POWER OF GRATITUDE

If the only prayer you said in your whole life is "thank you,"
that would suffice.
    —Meister Eckhart

Prior to achieving Findependence and starting his Victory Lap, Mike wasn't thrilled about how he was living his life. He felt like he was just killing time, waiting for eventual retirement while feeling stuck in a job he no longer loved. Every day it was the same routine. He and the Contessa would get up early, go to work, get home, make dinner, watch TV, then repeat the same cycle over and over. Days turned into weeks, weeks into months, months into years, and before they knew it they felt like they were among the walking dead.

Luckily, Mike has a pretty smart wife who could sense his unhappiness and she pushed him to do something about it before it destroyed him. Even though he would have to give up a good-paying job and resigning early would mean a reduced pension, she reminded him there were more important things in life than just having the ability to buy more stuff. Somewhere along the line Mike had forgotten this. But when he finally decided to set out on his Victory Lap, his attitude began to change and he started to see the world differently.

Over the years we become so focused on what we *think* we need to acquire to achieve happiness that we forget to be grateful for what we already have, what we've already accomplished, and what's really important. When we think about gratitude we're reminded of the old Persian proverb, "I wept because I had no shoes until I saw a man who had no feet." It's so easy to magnify our problems and lose sight of the many blessings for which we all have to be thankful. We must stop taking things for granted and realize what a great life we already have. Having gratitude is so powerful: it has the ability to transform your thinking from negative to positive, which in turn will enhance your well-being.

To increase your own sense of gratitude, it can be very helpful to create a list of all the things for which you're grateful. Your list will be unique to you and should contain all the important things in your life for which you're deeply grateful and that will assist you to face whatever you have to deal with today.

Mike's gratitude list looks like this:

- I'm grateful I was born in Canada, one of the greatest (nicest) countries in the world.
- I'm grateful to have married Melina, one of the most caring, loving people in the world. She continues to amaze me each and every day and I love having the opportunity to build a life and business together with her.
- I'm grateful for our three wonderful children and can't wait to see what great accomplishments they will achieve in the years ahead.
- I'm grateful I have found a second career that has given my life purpose and a high degree of personal satisfaction.
- I'm grateful that my friend Jonathan decided to partner with me in writing this book, which I know will help so many people.
- I'm grateful to be in a position to help others achieve happiness in finding their true passions, and to help take the fear out of retirement planning.

In addition to having a gratitude list, it's a good idea to start a gratitude journal. This will serve to train your brain to focus on the many positives in your life, the things that really count. Each day try to list at least three positive things that happened to you that day. It may be hard at first and there may be a great deal of repetition early on, but it will force your brain to review the tape from the last twenty-four hours and search out positive, meaningful events or people that you encountered, things you otherwise might have forgotten or taken for granted.

Over time you will start to see and appreciate the small things that add up to a happy life and realize how blessed you really are. Things like the taste of a good meal, going on a slow walk after dinner with your spouse, and taking the time to enjoy a sunset will take on an increased significance. Life is pretty good when you take the time to think about it. So whenever you start to feel anxiety, envy, or worry creeping in, you'll be able to pull out your gratitude list and remember what is really important in the grand scheme of things. Gratitude will win out every time.

HOW MUCH IS ENOUGH?
THE TALE OF THE MEXICAN FISHERMAN

Asked to define "wealthy," most financial advisers would probably define it in terms of money and their clients' ability to buy things that supposedly will make them happy. However, becoming wealthy is much more than having obtained a certain amount of money. True wealth is based on personal satisfaction and having the freedom to live life on your own terms. It's the kind of freedom Findependence gives you, and the satisfaction you gain from running a Victory Lap once you are financially independent.

An instructive example of true wealth can be found in the story of the Mexican fisherman, originally told by the German writer Heinrich Boll in 1963. Since then, it has been re-told and adapted by many. It's a classic tale about the general theme of living in the present, and the folly of forever "slaving and saving" today for the mirage of a single one-time-and-forever "retirement" in the far-off future. (All on the assumption that employers, pension managers, financial markets, health, spouses, and family will cooperate.) This apocryphal tale often finds its way into financial books, and it's a parable that never fails to amuse us, even after multiple readings. To us, it epitomizes the difference between working to live, and living to work.

The protagonist of this little fable is a humble fisherman. The antagonist is a rich American investment banker who visits the fisherman's pier located in a small coastal village of Mexico. A little boat with just one fisherman is docked by the pier. Inside the boat are several large yellowfin tuna. The American compliments the Mexican on the quality of his fish and asks how long it took to catch them.

"Only a little while," replies the Mexican.

The banker is curious as to why he didn't stay out longer to catch still more fish, and the fisherman replies that he has enough to support the immediate needs of his family.

The American then asks, "But what do you do with the rest of your time?"

The fisherman replies, "I sleep late, fish a little, play with my children, take siestas with my wife, Maria, stroll into the village each evening where I sip wine, and play guitar with my amigos. I have a full and busy life."

To this, the banker—who among other things possesses a Harvard MBA—scoffs incredulously. He tells the fisherman he should spend more time fishing and buy a bigger boat. "With the proceeds from the bigger boat, you could buy several boats; eventually you would have a fleet of fishing boats. Instead of selling your catch to a middleman you would sell directly to the processor, eventually opening your own cannery. You would control the product, processing, and distribution."

Of course, there's one small catch: to do all of this the fisherman would have to leave his small coastal fishing village, move to Mexico City and ultimately New York in order to run the thriving enterprise.

Dismayed, the fisherman asks how long all this would take. He's told fifteen or twenty years.

"But then what?" the fisherman persists.

The American laughs and says, "That's the best part. When the time is right you would announce an IPO and sell your company stock to the public and become very rich, you would make millions!"

"Millions—then what?"

"Why, then you would retire," the banker replies triumphantly, pointing out that the fisherman could then move to a small coastal fishing village in Mexico, sleep late every day, fish whenever he wished, play with his kids, take siestas with Maria, stroll to the village to sip wine in the evenings and play guitar with his amigos.

It's a killer punchline—though in real life the kids would have to be replaced with grandkids, the amigos would be long gone, and the odds are 50/50 that by then the beleaguered fisherman would be paying alimony to Maria. Even so, this story really resonates with us, and with almost anyone we know who has encountered it. This is because it clearly demonstrates what wealth is and isn't. It reminds us that true wealth has more to do with *feeling* wealthy rather than having accumulated a certain level of assets.

What constitutes feeling wealthy? How about having good health, having a congenial spouse, having a loving relationship with your family, having a few really close friends, having the freedom to spend time doing what you want to do when you want to do it? A wealthy man is content with what he has. If you want more than you have, you are not wealthy.

Throughout our lives, we have been taught that success is based on a person's net worth and the accumulation of things. We have been conditioned by the advertising industry to believe that buying a new car or the latest gadget will make us happy. But this happiness is fleeting and there is always a new advertisement about a better car, better gadgets, and all the other trinkets of modern society. We need to step back, clear our minds, and determine what is really important to us. We need to realize we may already have enough and become content with the life we are living now instead of the lifestyle being sold to us by advertisers.

What does having "enough" mean? It starts with having achieved sufficient financial freedom that we feel secure enough to choose meaningful work regardless of compensation. For Mike, enough means he can finally stop chasing happiness and contentment, as he already has it; he just didn't see it. He now knows he is richer than those who have more money but lack the understanding to enjoy what they have worked for.

Enough means having enough to live, enough to be happy, enough to chase your dreams. Now you can stop spending so much time making a living and focus solely on making a life, because you finally realize that you have enough.

The Final Chapter

How Would You Like Yours to Read?

Twenty years from now, you will be more disappointed by the things you didn't do, than by the things you did do. So throw off the bowlines. Sail away from the safe harbor. Catch the trade winds in your sails. Explore. Dream. Discover.
—Mark Twain

NO REGRETS: LIVE AN UNCOMMON LIFE

One of the saddest things that can happen to people is suddenly realizing in the twilight of their lives that they feel a great deal of regret over a life only half lived. Recently we read a book written by palliative care nurse Bronnie Ware. Over the years Ware had recorded the regrets of her dying patients, and she shared the information in her book *The Top Five Regrets of the Dying: A Life Transformed by the Dearly Departed*. According to the

book, the number one disappointment shared by Ware's patients was, "I wish I'd had the courage to live a life true to myself, not the life others expected of me." Many people follow the path that their parents or teachers thought would be best for them and, in so doing, they gave up their own personal dreams. They realize too late that they should have taken the more risky or the more fulfilling job, for example, but for whatever reason didn't.

This theme runs through a recently published book called *Sixty: The Beginning of the End, or the End of the Beginning?* by Ian Brown, who happens to be an acquaintance of Jonathan's. After noting his sixtieth birthday with a long post on Facebook, Brown kept a journal for his entire sixty-first year and the result seemed to encapsulate the dilemma of his generation: we all seem to be running out of time to achieve what we thought we were going to do when we graduated from college more than half a lifetime ago. It's even more poignant when you look at the relatively early deaths of some major creative artists who *did* live the life of their dreams, like Eagles co-founder Glenn Frey or the iconic David Bowie, who passed away at 67 and 69 respectively.

This theme also seems to tie into a Gallup poll that found 70 per cent of people hate their current job, according to the survey results published in a 2011 *Forbes* article. Clearly, something is not quite right here. For many people, dreams go unfulfilled because of earlier choices they made or avoided making. If you wish to prevent this kind of regret in your life, you need to start making the right choices so you can leave this world with peace of mind.

For example, changing from a job you don't like to one you love, even if it means earning less money, makes sense because the quality of your remaining life will improve. (Jonathan once took a $25,000 cut in pay in order to leave the lucrative field of public relations and re-enter the field of journalism, which he found much more satisfying. Over the years, he made up the short-term hit and then some, but the real benefit of finding a more congenial occupation cannot be measured in dollars and cents.)

The second most common regret in Ware's book was, "I wish I hadn't worked so hard." People deeply regretted spending so much of their lives at work, where the focus was primarily on making money. They wished they had spent more time with their family and friends, and they regretted taking life so seriously all the time. Along the same lines, a regret of Mike's—or maybe we should call it guilt—was when he looked back and realized he had spent the best years of his children's lives climbing the imaginary ladder of success at the Corp in pursuit of security for his family.

Always remember the greatest gift you can give to your family is the gift of your time, of you! Many of us tend to forget this; we are so busy just trying to survive that we end up investing most of our time in our jobs. Unfortunately, Mike can't go back and change things, but he, for one, plans on spending the rest of his life making up for lost time. The guilt will always be there, but he intends to bury it under many new experiences he plans to share with his family and the amazing memories they'll continue to make together.

The third most common regret was, "I wish I'd had the courage to express my feelings." Many people go through life with their opinions and emotions bottled up inside. They feel they can't say how they really feel because it might make them look weak. It's important to tell your kids and your spouse on a regular basis that you love them. There's nothing weak in doing that. Saying you love someone is one of the most impactful things you can say to another person, and it doesn't cost a cent.

The fourth most common regret was, "I wish I had stayed in touch with my friends." Long-term friends are priceless. Building these deep relationships takes time and it's a downright sin to let these connections slip away through neglect or feeling that you are too busy to maintain them. Make long-term relationships a priority in your life because they will pay off large whenever you need them.

The fifth most common regret is, "I wish I had let myself be happier." It's unfortunate that many people wake up and realize only late in life that happiness was always up to them to create. Real happiness depends on adopting a lifelong positive attitude. And, as we saw in the previous chapter, your happiness also depends not on pursuing some external ideal but on finding it within yourself. You are responsible for your own happiness, and the sooner you realize this, the sooner you'll be truly happy.

Statements like "I wish I had made more money" or "I wish I owned more things" didn't make it into the top five lifetime regrets. Puts things in perspective, doesn't it?

After reviewing the tapes of your life, you will probably find the most regret will flow from the risks that you did *not* take, the opportunities that you did *not* pursue, and the fears that you let control you because you didn't have the courage to face them. It's important to realize that fear inhibits us and prevents us from living a wonderful life. While we still have the time, we need to break free of our self-imposed fears; we have to get out of our comfort zone, stop playing it safe and take more risks. Stop being so focused on chasing and maintaining security, and instead focus on chasing opportunity. That's when a person really starts living. The saddest words you will ever hear are, "I could have been . . . if only I had . . . ."

For whatever reason, most people fail to live out their dreams. They remain in survivor mode waiting for something to happen that will change their lives for the better, but nothing ever seems to materialize. As the years go by, they become frustrated and bitter. If you want evidence of this just visit any retirement home and sit at the table occupied by the complainers. You can't miss it—it's the table with all the sour faces.

In her book *Silver Boxes: The Gift of Encouragement*, Florence Littauer described her father's lifelong desire to become a singer and the sad fact that he never became one. She said he died with the music within him. Not attempting to become the person you know you should be is like dying with the music still inside you.

It's a shame to simply endure and complain about life or to miss out on it altogether; instead, take risks and squeeze every bit out of life that you can. Our time on earth is way too short, or maybe it's better to think of it as too fast. We all know how it ends, so why not do some cool stuff while you still have the chance? And that's what your Victory Lap is for—living life to the maximum now that you're financially secure and while you're still young enough to enjoy it. Remember, each of us has the power to choose the kind of life we want to live. Choose to be happy or choose to live with regret; the choice is yours alone.

THE GREAT CIRCLE OF LIFE

Mike's father taught him a lot of basic lessons early in life: study hard, work hard, save your money, avoid debt, and take care of your family. He was the teacher and Mike the willing student. But now Mike finds that it is his mother who is filling in the remaining blanks, imparting some of the lessons his father never had the chance to teach him. His mother's recent journey from retirement home to the nursing home has been an eye opener: Mike is finally starting to understand that happiness and a sense of fulfillment come from within.

Things seem relatively meaningless when we come face to face with our ultimate destiny, which is apparent at every visit Mike makes to that nursing home. Looking back, there was a progression: each move his mother made—from detached house, to retirement home, to nursing home—resulted in a shrinking of her living space and a corresponding reduction in her possessions. Now she has only a few pieces of furniture left, pictures of her family that adorn the walls, and memories. You begin to realize that somewhere along the way things got messed up. Surely we were not born just to die, leaving a big pile of unused, discarded consumer junk behind. Why did we buy all that stuff in the first place?

When life is boiled down to its essentials, it becomes easy to separate what's important from what's not; you realize money is not the most important thing, nor are the items it allowed you to purchase over the course of your life. What's really important, what really matters, are the memories we created with our friends and families, and the lives we have touched and tried to help—all the people who hold a special place in our hearts.

Mike watches his mother sometimes when she sits staring blankly at a wall. He wonders what she's thinking about and on what meaningful moments in her life she is focused. One day he and the rest of us will be in her shoes, assuming we live that long. We'll review the tapes, judging whether we made a difference in other people's lives, living on our own memories. Whether we will be remembered, and how we will be remembered, is what really matters.

The thought of possibly living with some level of regret over lost dreams or missed opportunities is scary, so Mike made a promise to himself to invest the rest of his time on this planet chasing his own dreams, helping people in some fashion, and making wonderful memories with his wife, kids and, hopefully one day, grandchildren. Mike is running the awesome Victory Lap that he designed intentionally for himself.

IT'S YOUR STORY: WHY NOT WRITE A HAPPY ENDING?

Our job in this life is not to shape ourselves into some ideal we imagine we ought to be, but to find out who we already are and become it.
—*Steven Pressfield*

The tragedy of life is not death but what we let die inside of us while we live.
—*Norman Cousins*

Every year around Christmas, Mike looks forward to watching the movie adaptation of *A Christmas Carol*. It's based on the

Charles Dickens classic about the mean and miserable Ebenezer Scrooge, a money lender who constantly bullies his poor clerk, Bob Cratchit, and rejects his nephew Fred's wishes for a merry Christmas. Scrooge lives only for money, has no real friends or family, and cares only about his own well-being. As the story goes, on Christmas Eve Scrooge is visited by three ghosts that teach him the lessons of the Christmas spirit through his visions of Christmases past, present, and future; in each visit he sees either the negative consequences his miserly nature has created or the good tidings that others bring about through their love and kindness. Scrooge sees his future death: dying alone, with no one to mourn him. He has his money and his possessions, but nothing else. He finally understands why qualities like generosity and love are some of the most important things in life. He is grateful when he realizes he has a chance to redeem himself and change his future. This is the important message conveyed by the film: if Scrooge can change and improve his future life, then anyone can change theirs.

Imagine the satisfaction you could have if you arrived at the end of your days knowing that you did everything you possibly could have done in order to live the life you wanted. Put some thought into how your Victory Lap can help you do this, both for yourself and the people closest to you. Don't be like most people who finally figure out how to live while lying on their deathbed, suffering from regret.

The timing of *A Christmas Carol* is perfect for Mike as it puts him in the right frame of mind for the annual review he and the Contessa conduct at the end of December. It's a reminder of what's really important and what's not: that it's all about what a person accomplishes in life. Not in terms of making money or acquiring things, but how a person has helped and touched the souls of others. It's a reminder that we still have a last chance to be remembered as we want and that we need to start living that way today. All of us have control over how we are going to live from this day forward and the quality of your life will depend upon the choices you make each and every day. (And remember there's really only one day to do all these things, and that day is *today*.)

So somewhat like Scrooge, you can give yourself the power of choice, but in this case by achieving Findependence, which enables you to design the Victory Lap you want to live. It's not too late to choose optimism, action, and the pursuit of a life well lived. Do you like the way you are currently living? If your current job adds a lot of stress to your life, adopting a Victory Lap philosophy might be the answer you have been looking for—an escape route to a life and work that you find deeply fulfilling.

It's important to understand that the only risk bigger than starting a Victory Lap is staying in a stressful job that you dislike. How much stress does the job add to your life? How does it impact your relationship with your family and friends and your quality of life? Why become a work zombie doing a job you hate for money that you really don't need, half of which, for those in the top tax brackets, is taxed away? The government will thank you for your generous support of the treasury department, and your heirs may welcome a hefty inheritance, but what about the squandered life energy and relationships that could have instead been cultivated in a balanced Victory Lap?

Mind you, if you're fortunate enough to have a high-level corporate career for which you have real zest and passion, that's quite another matter. Your Victory Lap might allow you to continue to go down that same path but gradually reduce the number of days or hours you work. Perhaps you'd take your expertise to other Corps that could benefit from you being a board member or a consultant.

The networking opportunities that result would be part of a well-planned Victory Lap for these kinds of high achievers.

Think about all the wealthy people in the world who do not have to work, but who still choose to do so: Warren Buffett and Jimmy Pattison come to mind, both of whom have committed their late-life careers and the bulk of their wealth to philanthropy. The reason they continue to work is because they love what they are doing. Like them, we have no intention of retiring and our adventure is not over. This is something we should all strive for and Victory Lap will help get you there.

Why worry about your health or about running out of money when you can do something about it? People generally don't take charge of their own life because the easiest way to deal with change and all the anxieties that go with it is not to deal with it at all. We act this way to avoid responsibility and because we're not willing to make an effort. You need to be different and to take action.

So don't waste time fretting about things that don't matter. Instead, focus on the things that really matter—family, enjoyable work, health, and fun experiences. Your plan should be to squeeze out every last remaining ounce of life that you can. Don't squander your last chance to chase your dreams in Victory Lap. Get out of your comfort zone and really start living again. Stop playing it safe and start dreaming big, like when you were a kid. You're not too old to try something new, all you need is the courage to start. Believe us, you won't regret it!

We wrote this book for people who are not satisfied, and who want more. For the people who are saying to themselves, "Hey, I'm not done yet." By choosing to do a Victory Lap, you are willing to make changes to a story that is still only partially written. Why not write a happy ending for yourself? You can if you choose to! It's all up to you.

WHERE DO WE GO FROM HERE?

He who has a "why" to live can bear almost any "how."
— *Friedrich Nietzsche*

After reading this book, you can no doubt now see that we have all been seduced into believing that the traditional full-stop retirement is the answer for a wonderful life. After all, they tell us, isn't that the reason we worked so hard over the years, so one day we would be able to sit back and do nothing?

We've been culturally brainwashed to accept retirement as the answer to all our problems. We all bought into the deal: work hard for thirty-five years and then you can finally begin to enjoy a wonderful life in retirement. After reading this book you probably realize that retirement is a relatively new phenomenon. It's the carrot, an invented need, an artificial solution to a man-made problem that's in direct conflict with our natural instincts.

We have all been sold on the need to work hard and save like crazy over a long period of time, then to hit the brakes and do something inherently unnatural: retire. No wonder we are so stressed out. Work is an essential part of life: people need to be able to contribute, they need to interact and socialize, and they need to have a good reason for getting out of bed in the morning. Retirement is not the best answer for many.

If you think like us, it's okay to say you like to work; it's okay to stop doing what *they say* will make you happy, and do what *you know* will make you happy. Find work that makes life interesting and fun. Create a lifestyle based on some combination of work and play that gives you what you need. As we say on the cover, you want the flexibility to play while you work and to work while you play. If you've really designed your Victory Lap properly, you'll barely know the difference between work and play. Congenial work *is* play! Life doesn't have to be so difficult and unsatisfying, if you choose to be intentional and take steps to create a great life. Having the chance to pursue your true purpose, how can you argue with that? How can you lose?

Neither of us has even scratched the surface of what we want to be, what we wish to achieve, and what we want to contribute—and that's what gets us up each and every morning. Who knows what new ideas and possibilities will come to us during our respective Victory Laps? The beauty of being in Victory Lap is that now we control our own days and set our own agenda. We don't do anything we don't want to do, and that puts a big smile on our faces!

So there you have it, a new approach to maximizing the quality of your remaining years. You have paid your dues, you have met your responsibilities to your family, and now it is your time to create that lifestyle you always dreamed about. You can make it happen if you want to; you are more than capable, and the decision is yours and yours alone. So what are you waiting for?

Acknowledgements

The authors wish to thank the following people for their contributions, knowledge, and other help in creating this book.

MIKE:

First and foremost I would like to thank my beautiful wife, Melina, who I affectionately call "The Contessa," for standing beside me while I went a little crazy writing this book. She is my rock, the love of my life, and I dedicate this book, or at least my portion of it, to her.

To my father, Stanley Drak, who taught me my first Victory Lap lessons, and to my mother, Viola Drak, who continues to show me the way.

To my kids, Doug, Danny, and Austin, for encouraging me and for helping me solve all of the many computer problems I encountered while writing this book.

To Ernie Zelinski, whose book *How to Retire Happy, Wild, and Free* motivated me to start on this journey. Ernie has been and continues to be a great mentor to both Jonathan and me. We are lucky to have him in our corner, as can be seen in the Foreword he graciously penned for this book.

To Tom Deans for taking the time to show us the ropes and for encouraging us to take the book on the seminar circuit.

Special thanks to Robert Ott for helping us come up with a great name for our book!

And lastly, to my co-author and friend, Jonathan: Writing a book was a lot tougher than I thought. Yes, I know you warned me about it, but now the hard work is behind us and the fun starts!

JONATHAN:

To my wife, Ruth, and daughter, Helen, who keep hoping every book will be my last. They're my reason for getting up in the morning.

Thanks to our editor, Karen Milner, who I finally got to work with after a few earlier almost-deals in our previous publishing incarnations.

To Steve Nease, for creating the compelling cartoons that will provide some comic relief during the reader's jog through the pages of *Victory Lap Retirement*.

A special thanks to "Eagle Eyes" Christopher Cottier, the best technical editor around when it comes to financial books. And to David Chilton, whose generosity to fellow authors continues to astound.

And last but certainly not least, to my co-author, Mike, whose enthusiasm for this project overcame my initial doubts about attempting yet another book.

Order the prequel!
FINDEPENDENCE DAY
How to Achieve Financial Independence:
While You're Still Young Enough to Enjoy It
by Jonathan Chevreau

You've read a lot in *Victory Lap Retirement* about one of Jonathan's previous books, *Findependence Day*. This "personal finance novel" is a precursor to the idea of Victory Lap and, in fact, we believe that achieving financial independence is a prerequisite to running your own Victory Lap.

For more information on Jonathan's book (available in both U.S. and Canadian editions), or to purchase copies, please visit:

www.findependenceday.com

- Information about the book
- Reviews and interviews on *Findependence Day*
- Preview of the first chapter
- Link to the **Financial Independence Hub**, a portal with a wealth of information on how you can plan for and achieve Findependence

www.findependencehub.com

Also available are two editions of a short Kindle e-book, *A Novel Approach to Financial Independence*, summarizing the plot of *Findependence Day* and the major financial lessons learned by the characters. You can find the U.S. edition at Amazon.com and Canadian edition at Amazon.ca.

To contact Jonathan Chevreau directly, please email: jonathan@findependencehub.com

LEAVE THE RAT RACE BEHIND AND RUN YOUR OWN VICTORY LAP!

Mike Drak is living the dream, running his own Victory Lap and making it his mission to help others do the same.

If you're interested in Mike's life planning and consulting services, feel free to contact him at:

michael.drak@yahoo.ca

Mike and Jonathan are also available for speaking enagagements and seminars and would be delighted to share their knowledge and enthusiasm about Victory Lap and financial independence with your group.

Please visit the Victory Lap website for more information, and feel free to join our community—we'd love to hear your stories!

www.victorylapretirement.ca

About the Authors

MICHAEL DRAK is a thirty-eight-year veteran of the financial services industry and lives with his wife, Melina (also known affectionately as "The Contessa"), in Toronto. He started his own Victory Lap in 2014 and is busy helping others transition into their own personal versions. In addition to mentoring others, he gives speeches and seminars to groups across the country and cultivates and maintains the Victory Lap community at www.victorylapretirement.ca.

JONATHAN CHEVREAU is a veteran financial columnist, blogger, and author. He was personal finance columnist for the *Financial Post* (1993-2012), and editor-in-chief of *MoneySense* magazine (2012-14). Since declaring his Findependence Day in 2014, he has been blogging for the Motley Fool, Financial Post, and MoneySense.ca, and launched the Financial Independence Hub in 2014, a website that covers the topic from a North American perspective. He has published US and Canadian editions of his financial novel *Findependence Day*, and is also the author of *The Wealthy Boomer* and several editions of *Smart Funds*.